JAN **HENDERIKSE**

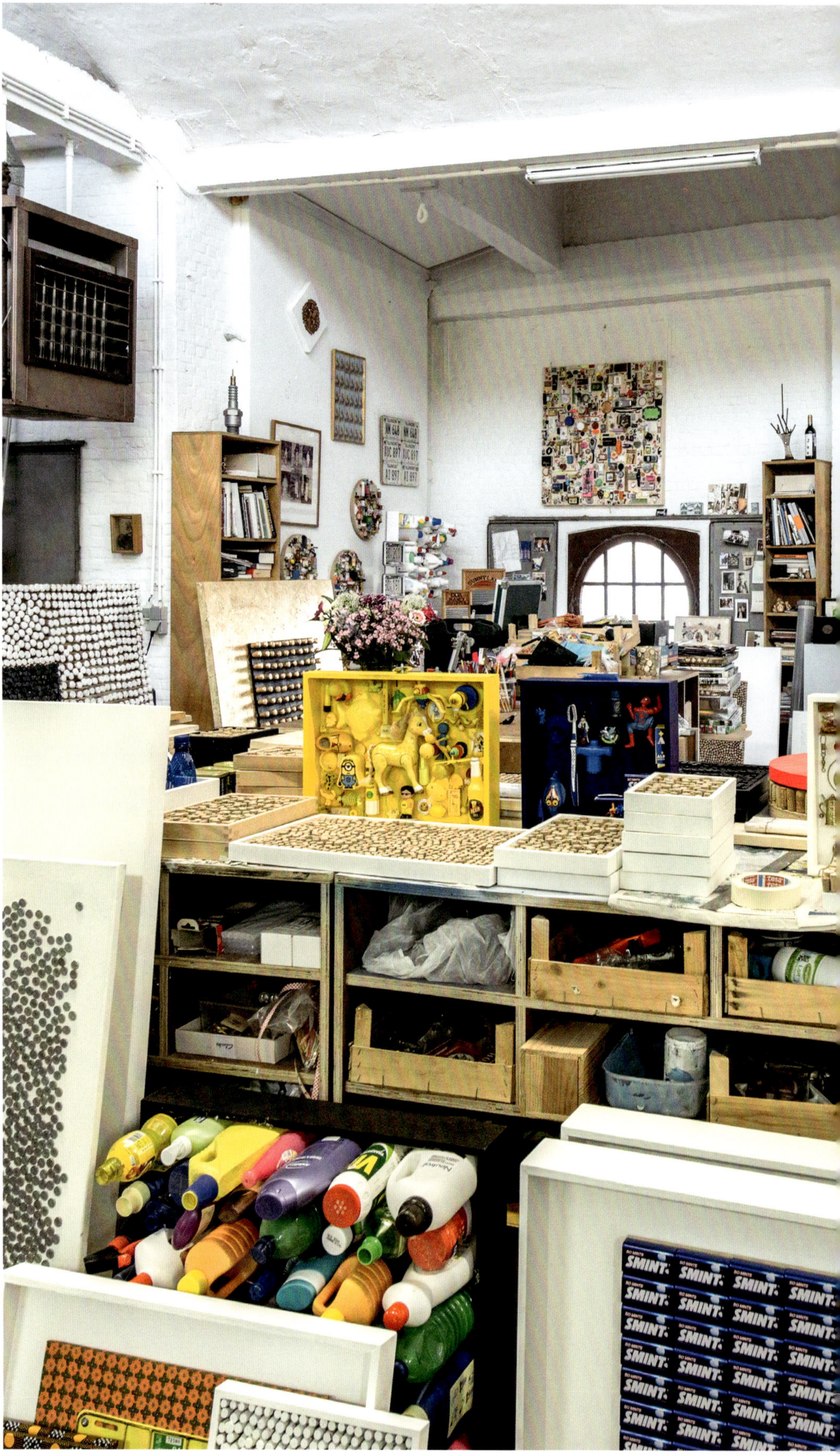
SMINT

# JAN
# HENDERIKSE

ZWISCHEN | BETWEEN

**ZERO**

UND | AND

**POP ART**

ARBEITEN | WORKS 1967 – 2017

**KERBER** ART

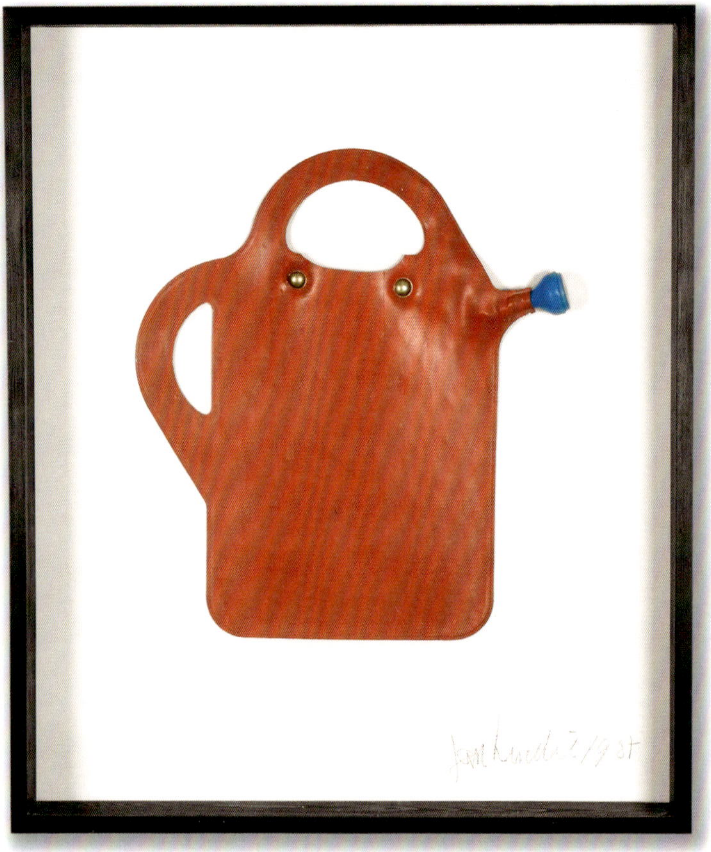

*Giesskanne*, 1987

# „ZUVIEL IST NICHT GENUG!“

Antoon Melissen im Gespräch mit Jan Henderikse

Antoon Melissen: *Die Nederlandse Informele Groep [Niederländische Informelle Gruppe] wurde 1958 gegründet. Welche Erinnerungen verbindest du mit dieser Zeit bezüglich der Formierung einer Gruppe und deines Starts als bildender Künstler?*

*Jan Henderikse:* Im Prinzip ergab sich die Gründung der Informellen Gruppe aus sehr praktischen Überlegungen. Vor allem hofften wir, dass es einfacher sein würde, als Gruppe ausgestellt zu werden. Zuvor war es mir in dem Jahr gelungen, uns unsere erste Gruppenausstellung in der Studenten-Cafeteria der Polytechnischen Hochschule in Delft zu verschaffen. Man muss bedenken, dass mit Ausnahme von Cor de Nobels Galerie .31 in Dordrecht die offizielle Kunstszene in Holland nichts mit uns zu tun haben wollte. De Nobel kam 1958 nach Delft, um Jan Schoonhoven zu einer Einzelausstellung einzuladen – Ich war damals zufällig gerade zu Besuch bei Schoonhoven. Es war typisch für Jan, dass er sagte, „klar, ich mach' das, aber lass' den Jungen hier erstmal machen.“ So hatte ich, dank Jan Schoonhoven, 1958 meine erste Einzelausstellung. Es waren darin ein paar wirklich gute informelle Arbeiten enthalten. In jenen Tagen habe ich noch mit Fassadenfarbe gearbeitet, Reste, die ich von einem Farbengeschäft in Delft erhielt. In der Galerie waren auf den Bodenfliesen unter den Bildern noch Tropfen von Farbe – so frischgemalt waren sie! Schoonhoven hat mich darin bestärkt, mit der Kunst weiterzumachen – er hat in meinen Arbeiten irgendetwas gesehen. Mehr als einmal schenkte er mir Stapel von Papier, weil ich es mir kaum leisten konnte, Materialien zu kaufen. Mein erster Besuch bei Jan und Anita Schoonhoven machte auf mich riesigen Eindruck. Ein Künstler mit eigenem Atelier – das war für mich wirklich eine komplett andere Welt. Und doch kam Schoonhoven aus dem Arbeitermilieu. Keiner von uns hatte irgendwelche Kontakte zur Kunstwelt, wir hatten keinen, der für uns Strippen ziehen und uns unterstützen konnte. Wir haben uns alles selbst aufgebaut. Während der Zeit der Gruppe *Nul* war es übrigens genauso: Museen und Galerien hatten keinerlei Interesse an unseren Arbeiten. Es war natürlich in erster Linie Henk Peeters, der sehr aktiv Kontakte knüpfte – seine Schreibmaschine stand nie still. Ohne ihn wären viele Initiativen nie in Gang gekommen.

*Du hast recht schnell, 1959, die Niederlande verlassen. Was veranlasste dich auszuwandern?*

Ich wollte Holland immer schon verlassen. Ich konnte dort nicht so recht meine Nische finden, und es war mir auch nicht möglich, ernsthaft zu arbeiten. Deshalb wollte ich auswandern, um zur Abwechslung einmal *richtige* Kunst zu machen. Doch hatten wir um 1958 herum kaum eine Ahnung davon, was in anderen Ländern los war. Künstler-Freund Henk Peeters hatte ein Abonnement der Zeitschrift *Das Kunstwerk*, dadurch konnten wir uns ein wenig auf dem Laufenden halten. Ich hörte manchmal ein paar Dinge durch Bram Bogart, der auch aus Delft kam und in den frühen 1950ern nach Paris gezogen war. Und Anita Schoonhoven war eine Freundin der Bildhauerin Lotti van der Gaag, die ebenfalls seit 1950 in Paris lebte. Aber das hat nicht wirklich viel gebracht – in jenen Tagen war man in Holland richtig isoliert.

*Du hast mehrere Jahre in Düsseldorf verbracht. Hast du Düsseldorf aufgrund des Umfelds der deutschen ZERO-Künstler ausgewählt?*

Nein, keineswegs. Ich bin 1959 ausgewandert und ging erst nach Köln, im späteren Verlauf des Jahres dann nach Düsseldorf. In der Vergangenheit hatte ich in Deutschland als Reiseführer auf diesen Urlaubsdampfern auf dem Rhein gearbeitet, so war ich mit der Gegend ein wenig vertraut. Ich hoffte, dass der Umzug Bewegung in mein Leben bringen würde, und so war es auch. Nachdem ich Delft verlassen hatte, habe ich nie wieder gemalt – es war ein wirklich radikaler Bruch. In Köln begegnete ich Günther Uecker und durch Günther fand ich ein Atelier in Düsseldorf. Joseph Beuys und Gotthard Graubner waren meine neuen Nachbarn – Beuys hat die Tatsache, dass ich den schönsten Raum hatte, immer gehasst. Wir hatten aber kaum Kontakt zueinander, unsere Welten waren so weit auseinander. Er zeichnete damals noch und ich arbeitete bereits an meinen ersten Assemblagen. Ich machte in Düsseldorf endlose Spaziergänge mit meiner Frau Idi am Rhein entlang und nahm alles mit, was ich interessant fand, selbst Dinge, die ans Ufer gespült worden waren. Während dieser Zeit war mein Atelier bis unters Dach vollgepackt, und ich musste abends immer einen Weg frei räumen, wenn wir ins Bett gehen wollten. Wo wir gerade von Assemblagen sprechen: Als ich achtzehn war und noch in Amsterdam lebte, befestigte ich bereits alle Alltagsgegenstände, die ich verwendete, auf Platten. Das war 1955. Doch was macht man damit, wenn man achtzehn Jahre alt ist? Ich habe natürlich alles weggeschmissen. Eine entsetzliche Schande!

*Kannst du mir ein wenig über deine Kontakte um 1960 erzählen, über die Menschen, die du in Düsseldorf kennengelernt hast?*

Günther Uecker wohnte in Düsseldorf gleich um die Ecke von uns. Wir sprachen täglich mit ihm und waren während dieser Jahre gut befreundet. Uecker stellte seine Arbeiten gemeinsam mit Heinz Mack und Otto Piene aus, doch eigentlich hatten wir beide viel mehr gemeinsam. Auch der Düsseldorfer Galerist Alfred Schmela kam öfter vorbei. Ich ging meistens zusammen mit Uecker zu den Eröffnungen in Schmelas Galerie. Tatsächlich sah ich auch viele Ausstellungen außerhalb von Düsseldorf. *Monochrome*

*Malerei* in Leverkusen – dort begegnete ich Lucio Fontana – Yves Kleins Ausstellung *Monochrome und Feuer* in Krefeld und Christos Installation gestapelter Ölfässer im Kölner Hafen – das war auch 1961. Und natürlich Manzoni. Ich hatte seine Arbeiten bereits 1958 in Rotterdam gesehen, zusammen mit Jan Schoonhoven. Für uns war es wirklich ein Schock, Arbeiten zu sehen, die so provokativ waren. Jan war von der Ordnung in Manzonis Arbeiten sehr beeindruckt. Und natürlich war alles weiß, reines Weiß.

*Deine Arbeiten aus der Nul-Periode unterscheiden sich ziemlich signifikant von den anderen. Worin bestand aus deiner Sicht der verbindende Faktor?*

Das kann ich durch eine schöne Geschichte erläutern. Wir holten eines Tages Jan Schoonhoven in Delft ab, in einem 2CV, und fuhren alle nach Trier zur Eröffnung der Ausstellung *Avantgarde 61*. Es gibt davon noch ein Foto – von uns bei der Eröffnung in formellen Anzügen. Alle vier von uns konnten affektiertes Getue nicht ausstehen – die Art von Prätentionen und Attitüden, die man von Künstlern kennt, diesen bohemehaften Typen, die ihre Hände gezielt mit Farbe bespritzen und *dann* auf eine Eröffnung gehen. Da waren wir uns alle einig. Mit Armando verstand ich mich auf Anhieb. Wenn man heute die Manifeste von damals liest, erscheint das alles so schrecklich ernst und theoretisch ausformuliert, doch haben Armando und ich uns dabei kaputtgelacht, wenn wir uns Slogans ausdachten wie ‚Kreativität läuft in einem vernünftigen Anzug herum'. Ich war übrigens am eigentlichen Verfassen der Manifeste nicht beteiligt. Jan Schoonhoven hatte im Grunde dazu dieselbe Einstellung wie ich: ‚Lass' die Typen doch machen, was sie wollen, es hat eigentlich nichts mit mir zu tun', so sah er es mehr oder weniger. Wir saßen nicht alle den ganzen Tag herum und theoretisierten, dazu waren wir vom gedanklichen Ansatz her viel zu nüchtern. Zumindest war ich das. Aber wir teilten die Art zu denken, unabhängig davon wie unterschiedlich unsere Arbeiten waren.

*Wie blickst du von heute aus zurück auf die Nul-Periode?*

Naja, wie sehr ‚*Nul*' war ich eigentlich tatsächlich? Im Grunde war für mich *Nul* eher ein Vehikel. Ich gehörte dazu und zugleich auch nicht. Man muss auch beachten, dass *Nul* kein Club mit eigenem Briefpapier oder ähnliches war: Aus der Informellen Gruppe hat sich einfach etwas entwickelt, das dann zu *Nul* wurde. Viele stellen sich oft etwas Rigides vor, doch passieren viele Dinge ziemlich organisch. So wurden auch Konzepte für Ausstellungen gemacht: Es wurde viel geredet, und dann plötzlich hatte man die besten Ideen. So wie auch für die erste *Nul*-Ausstellung in Amsterdam 1962 – wir diskutierten darüber tatsächlich viel mit Günther Uecker und Yves Klein. Meine ursprüngliche Idee bestand darin, zwanzig Kisten Bier von der obersten Stufe der wunderschönen Marmortreppe im Stedelijk Museum hinunterzuschütten. Ich sah sie direkt vor mir, diese fantastische Schaumschicht, die den gesamten Museumsboden bedeckt. Und ich stand mit der Firma *Braun* wegen einer Kammer mit Blitzvorrichtung am Museumsausgang in Verbindung, die verursacht hätte, dass einem vier Tage lang Punkte vor den Augen flirren. Mit anderen Worten, echte ‚Kunst, die man mit nach Hause nimmt'! All diese Pläne wurden abgelehnt. Willem Sandberg sagte, ‚hast du den Verstand verloren?' Ich hatte sogar eine offizielle Erklärung von einem Augenarzt, dass es keinen Schaden anrichten würde. Der Arzt war übrigens Kettenraucher, denn die Zigarettenschachteln für die Assemblage, die ich 1962 im Stedelijk Museum ausstellte, kamen von ihm. Aber es stimmt, dass ich lange Zeit nichts mehr mit *Nul* zu tun haben wollte, was, nebenbei bemerkt, auch für Armando galt. Immer dieselben Anekdoten, und immer und immer wieder erklären zu müssen, worum es dabei genau ging. Ein aussichtsloser Kampf. Es ist tatsächlich unbegreiflich, dass die Holländer so viel Zeit dafür brauchten, dieser Periode Aufmerksamkeit zu widmen.

*1968, also nachdem sich die Gruppe* Nul *aufgelöst hatte, hattest du eine Einzelausstellung im Stedelijk Museum mit dem* Titel Jan Henderikse Uses Common Cents *[im Englischen ein Wortspiel zwischen ‚gewöhnliche Cents verwenden' und, gesunden Menschenverstand gebrauchen'].*

*‚Uses common sense' – ‚gesunden Menschenverstand gebrauchen' – spricht daraus noch immer der Geist von Nul?*

Ich hatte immer schon die Einstellung, dass man als Künstler seinen Verstand gebrauchen sollte, das ist nicht spezifisch für *Nul*. Marcel Duchamp hat es so formuliert: *‚bête comme un peintre'*, dumm wie ein Maler. Künstler sollten nicht zu viel über ihre eigene Arbeit philosophieren, das führt nur zu Problemen und Unsinn. Ich habe immer eine Nähe zu Duchamp empfunden in Bezug auf die Kombination, ernsthafte Arbeiten zu produzieren, ohne sich allzu wichtig zu nehmen. Duchamp war ein Meister des Selbstwiderspruchs, der immer wieder Spannungen geschürt hat. Das kann man auch in seinem Werk erkennen: Jeder Schritt ist eine Überraschung. Wim Beeren, in den 1980ern der Direktor des Stedelijk Museums, hat dies auch über meine Arbeiten gesagt – dass ich so unberechenbar sei. Mach' das, was dir gefällt, ob es in ein bestimmtes Muster hineinpasst oder nicht. Viele Künstler machen einfach immer auf dieselbe vertraute Weise weiter, nach dem Motto, nur keinen Staub aufwirbeln, nur nicht zu viele Veränderungen zulassen, weil es alles schiefgehen könnte. Für mich ist das der Tod. Ich wollte mich nie anpassen, ich könnte es nicht einmal. Was Wim Beeren meinte ist, dass die Leute von mir eine Assemblage erwarten, aber stattdessen die niederländische Nationalhymne als *mein* Kunstwerk erhalten, oder eine Installation von Cola-Flaschen. Das macht die Leute wütend, weil sie es nicht verstehen – es läuft ihren Erwartungen zuwider.

*Du hast Marcel Duchamp erwähnt.*
*Wie denkst du über das konzeptuelle Element in deiner eigenen Arbeit?*

Ich habe immer geglaubt, dass Kunst wirklich mehr eine Idee als ein Gegenstand ist. Ich denke. Ich habe mal eine Ausstellung konzipiert, in der ich plante, keine der Bestandteile selbst zu machen und die ich mir nicht einmal anschauen wollte. Vielleicht geht das zu weit – das wäre *zu* konsistent. Meine Installationen aus Obst- und Bierkisten von 1962 sind natürlich die Originalarbeiten. Doch ist der springende Punkt die Idee, nicht diese eine ursprüngliche Fassung. Vergiss' die Patina, vergiss' die alte Signatur, vergiss' die Originalarbeit: Der Wert der späteren Versionen der Installationen liegt irgendwo in der Mitte von alldem, und sie sind tatsächlich genauso einmalig wie die Originalfassung. Ich arbeitete 1959 schon mit Obst-, Gemüse- und Bierkisten, und habe meine ersten großen Installationen in meinem Atelier in dem Jahr realisiert. Ich habe sie erst 1962 gezeigt, erst im Stedelijk Museum und später in der Antwerpener Ausstellung *Anti-Peinture*. Wenn man zurückblick, erweist sich die Idee tatsächlich als stärker als die eine, für sich genommene Umsetzung.

*Du hast zuvor über eine gemeinsame Art des Denkens gesprochen. Und doch hast du an der zweiten* Nul-Ausstellung *in Amsterdam 1965 nicht teilgenommen.*

Das stimmt. Genau gesagt, bin ich 1964 ausgestiegen, weil ich an der *Nul/ZERO*-Ausstellung im Gemeente Museum in Den Haag 1964 nicht teilgenommen habe. Jan Schoonhoven und ich haben zwar über die Ausstellung korrespondiert, aber ich war zu dem Zeitpunkt bereits darüber hinaus. Es war alles ein wenig zu ernst, zu weiß, zu clean und ‚*ZERO*-haft' geworden. In den frühen Jahren war das anders. Die niederländischen Künstler hatten ihre eigene klare Identität, die dem Idealismus entgegenstand. Ganz anders als die Deutschen, wirklich stärker mit beiden Beinen auf dem Boden. Mir wurde das ein wenig zu ‚rein und hoch'. Ich habe dennoch 1966 einen Vorschlag für *ZERO on Sea* eingereicht, da mich die Idee von Kunst im öffentlichen Raum immer schon extrem angesprochen hat. Wenn ich zurückblicke, kann man einen deutlichen Unterschied zur deutschen *ZERO*-Gruppe feststellen, zu den Lichtinstallationen von Otto Piene, beispielsweise. Ich hatte einen Entwurf für einen Raum, der aus Bierkisten gebaut ist, entwickelt, mit einer Glühbirne in jeder Flasche. Die Glühbirnen sollten wie verrückt ständig an- und ausflackern, am besten natürlich nach dem Zufallsprinzip, nicht alle zur gleichen Zeit. Ich habe immer schon Mengen, Massen, vorzugsweise von Alltagsgegenständen, geliebt. Es ist provokativ, aber auch wunderschön, so wie dicht gedrängte Tribünen bei einem Baseball-Spiel wunderschön sind. Es ist im klassischen Sinn des Worts Dekoration, obwohl es mit Gegenständen zu tun hat, die andere vielleicht banal finden. Anders als viele andere Künstler, nebenbei bemerkt, halte ich ‚Dekoration' nicht für ein Schimpfwort!

*Arman hat auch mit Alltagsgegenständen und –materialien gearbeitet. Welchen Bezug haben deine Arbeiten aus der Nul-Periode mit denen von Arman?*

Ich sah Armans *Poubelles* das erste Mal in Paris. Die Arbeiten haben auf mich großen Eindruck gemacht. Dass man den Inhalt einer Mülltonne in ein Plexiglas-Gehäuse hineinstopft – viel radikaler, so dachte ich, konnte es nicht werden. Ich arbeitete ebenfalls mit allem, was mir über den Weg lief, aber ich hatte den Eindruck, dass in meinen Arbeiten mehr ‚Auswahl' zu finden war als in denen von Arman. Kunst zu machen ohne Technik, ohne jegliche Technik – das habe ich enorm bewundert, obwohl Armans Arbeiten oft viel durchkomponierter sind als meine. Gerade erst kürzlich habe ich gehört, dass er tatsächlich ziemlich selektiv vorgegangen ist, bevor diese Plexiglas-Kästen mit Müll verschlossen wurden. Ich sage nie etwas über meine eigenen Arbeiten. Dafür muss man sich an die Kunsthistoriker halten. Dennoch glaube ich, dass meine Arbeiten intuitiver, weniger konstruiert sind. Arman, ich selbst, aber auch Christo, Armando und natürlich Daniel Spoerri – so viele Leute suchten damals in gewöhnlichen Gegenständen nach dem ‚Eigentlichen', und doch haben es alle auf ihre eigene Weise gefunden. Günther Uecker hat mich einmal sehr höflich gefragt, ob er eine Arbeit mit Korken machen könne, so wie ich sie damals viel produzierte. Aber natürlich sah seine Arbeit ganz anders aus als meine, wirklich durchkomponiert, in Reihen gegliedert – ich würde das nie so machen. Der koreanische Künstler Nam June Paik hat einmal gesagt, dass Fernsehen eine solch neue und dramatische Form der Unterhaltung gewesen sei, dass es Künstlern gestattet habe, zur Produktion langweiliger und monotoner Arbeiten zurückzukehren. Vielleicht ist das gar keine so abwegige Vorstellung. Ich arbeite am liebsten mit alltäglichen Dingen, die andere völlig uninteressant finden oder gänzlich übersehen. Ausrangierte Fotos, Korken, Münzen, Nummernschilder, was auch immer. Wenn ich darauf zurückblicke, ist das wirklich eine konstante Linie in meiner Arbeit, tatsächlich bis zum heutigen Tag. Es stellt sich dann plötzlich heraus, dass all diese gewöhnlichen Gegenstände tatsächlich sehr interessant sind. Ich habe es zuvor schon oft gesagt: Mich interessiert alles, was Menschen bewegt. *Alles*. Vorzugsweise in großen Mengen. Je mehr, desto besser, zu viel ist nicht genug! Das erfasst es für mich wirklich am besten.

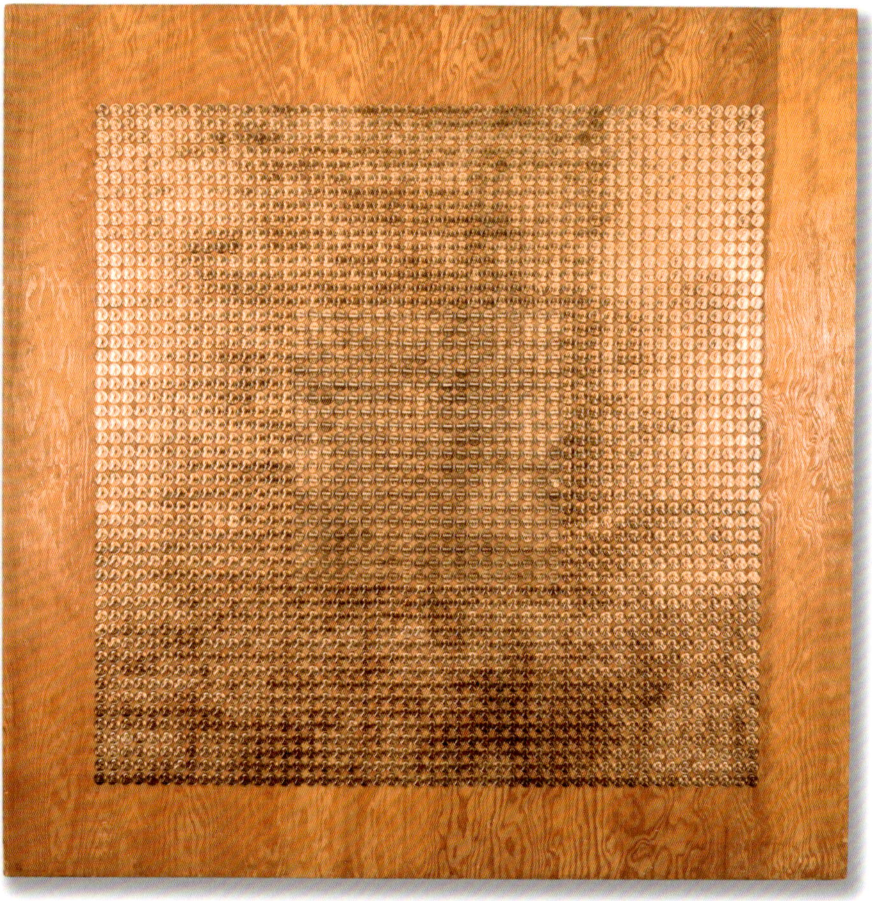

*Untitled*, 1968

# "TOO MUCH IS NOT ENOUGH!"

Antoon Melissen in conversation with Jan Henderikse

Antoon Melissen: ***The Dutch Informal Group was founded in 1958. How do you remember those years, in terms of forming a group, but also of your start as a visual artist?***

***Jan Henderikse:*** Actually the founding of the Informal Group came out of very practical considerations: mostly we were hoping that as a group it would be easier to get exhibited. Earlier that year I'd managed to get us our first group show at the student cafeteria of the Delft Polytechnic. Don't forget that the official art circuit in the Netherlands didn't want anything to do with us, with the exception of Cor de Nobel's Galerie .31 in Dordrecht. De Nobel came to Delft in 1958 to invite Jan Schoonhoven to put on a solo exhibition; I just happened to be visiting Schoonhoven at the time. It was so like Jan to say, 'sure, I'll do it, but let this kid do one first'. And so I had my first solo show in 1958, thanks to Jan Schoonhoven. There were really good Informal works in it. In those days I was still using house paint, left-overs I'd get from a paint shop in Delft. There were drops of paint on the floor tiles under the paintings in the gallery – that's how brand-new those pieces were! Schoonhoven encouraged me to continue with art – he saw something in my work. And he gave me stacks of paper on more than one occasion, because I could hardly afford buying materials. My first visit to Jan and Anita Schoonhoven made a huge impression on me. An artist with a studio – for me it was really a whole other world. And yet Schoonhoven was from a working-class background. Neither of us had any contacts whatsoever in the art world, nobody to pull strings and help us out. We set everything up ourselves. It was the same during the *Nul* Group period, by the way: museums and galleries had no interest at all in our work. It was primarily Henk Peeters, of course, who was very active in making contacts – his typewriter was never still. Without him many initiatives would never have got off the ground.

*You left the Netherlands fairly soon, in 1959.*
*What was behind your emigration?*

To get out of the Netherlands was what I'd always wanted! I couldn't really find my niche in the Netherlands, and I wasn't able to do any serious work either. That's why I wanted to emigrate, to produce *real* art for a change. And yet around 1958 we barely had any idea of what was going on in other countries. Artist-friend Henk Peeters had a subscription to the journal *Das Kunstwerk*, so we were able to keep up to date a little bit. I'd hear things sometimes through Bram Bogart, who was also from Delft and had moved to Paris in the early 1950s. And Anita Schoonhoven was a friend of the sculptor Lotti van der Gaag, who'd also been living in Paris since 1950. But it really didn't amount to much; in the Netherlands you were really isolated in those days.

*You spent several years in Düsseldorf.*
*Did you choose Düsseldorf because of the circle*
*around the German ZERO artists?*

No, absolutely not. I left in 1959, going first to Cologne and later that year to Düsseldorf. In the past I'd worked as a tour guide on those holiday boats on the German Rhine, so I was a little familiar with the area.

I hoped the move would shake things up, and actually it did. Once I left Delft, I never painted again – it was really a radical break. In Cologne I met Günther Uecker and through Günther I found a studio in Düsseldorf. Joseph Beuys and Gotthard Graubner were my new neighbours, and Beuys always hated the fact that I had the nicest space. But we had hardly any contact with each other; our worlds were so far apart. He was still drawing at the time and I was already working on my first assemblages. I'd take endless walks with my wife, Idi, along the Rhine in Düsseldorf, and I'd bring back anything I found interesting, even things that had washed up on the banks. My studio was packed to the rafters during that period, and I always had to clear a path in the evening when we wanted to go to bed. Speaking of assemblages, when I was 18 and living in Amsterdam, I was already sticking all the everyday things I used onto panels. That was in 1955. But what do you do with that when you're 18 years old? I threw it all away, of course. A terrible shame!

*Can you talk a little bit about your contacts around 1960, the people you met in Düsseldorf?*

Günther Uecker lived around the corner from us in Düsseldorf; we talked with him every day and we were good friends during those years. Uecker would exhibit his work with Heinz Mack and Otto Piene, but actually things clicked a lot better between the two of us. And the Düsseldorf gallery owner Alfred Schmela also dropped by frequently. I usually went to the openings at Schmela's gallery with Uecker. I also saw a lot of exhibitions outside Düsseldorf, as it happens. *Monochrome Malerei* in Leverkusen – that's where I met Lucio Fontana – Yves Klein's *Monochrome und Feuer* exhibition in Krefeld, and Christo's installation of stacked oil drums in the harbour of Cologne – that was in 1961 as well. And Manzoni, of course. I'd already seen his work in Rotterdam in 1958, with Jan Schoonhoven. For us it was really a shock to see work that was *that* provocative. Jan was hugely impressed by the order in Manzoni's work. And of course everything was white, pure white!

*Your works from the* Nul *period differ rather significantly from the anothers. What was the unifying factor, in your view?*

I can illustrate that with a nice story. We picked up Jan Schoonhoven in Delft one day, in a 2CV, and we all drove to Trier, to the opening of the exhibition *Avantgarde 61*. There's still a photo of that, of us at the opening in formal suits. All four of us hated affectation – the kind of pretensions and attitudes you'd get from artists, those bohemian types who'd deliberately splatter paint on their hands and *then* go to an opening. On that we all agreed. I really clicked with Armando. If you read the manifestos of the time now, it all seems so terribly serious and theoretically worked out, and yet Armando and I would be laughing our heads off making up slogans like 'creativity goes about dressed in a proper suit'. I wasn't involved in the writing of the manifestos, by the way. Jan Schoonhoven actually felt the same way about it as I did: 'Let's let those guys do what they like; it's really nothing to do with me' was more or less the way he looked at it. We weren't all sitting around all day theorizing; we were much too sober-minded for that. At least I was. But we did share a way of thinking. However different our works were.

*How do you look back on the* Nul *period?*

Yes, how '*Nul*' was I, really? Actually, for me *Nul* was more a vehicle. I was part of it, and yet I wasn't. And don't forget that *Nul* wasn't a club with it's own stationary or anything like that: something just evolved out of the Informal Group that became *Nul*. People often imagine something very rigid, but actually many things happen quite organically. And that's the way plans for exhibitions were made: lots of talking and then suddenly you'd get the best ideas. Like for the first *Nul* exhibition in Amsterdam, in 1962 – we discussed that a lot with Günther Uecker and Yves Klein, as it happens. My initial idea was to toss 20 crates of beer from the top of that beautiful marble staircase at the Stedelijk Museum. I could see it all, this fantastic layer of foam all over the museum floor. And I was in touch with the company *Braun* about a cabin with flash equipment at the museum exit, so you'd have spots in front of your eyes for four days. Real 'art you take home with you', in other words! All those plans were rejected. 'Are you out of your mind?' Willem Sandberg said. I even had an official statement from an eye doctor that it wouldn't do any harm. A chain smoker, that doctor, by the way, because the cigarette packs for the assemblage I exhibited at the Stedelijk Museum in 1962 came from him. But it's true I didn't want to have anything more to do with *Nul* for a long time, and neither did Armando, incidentally. Always the same anecdotes, and always having to explain, over and over, exactly what it was about. A losing battle. It's incomprehensible, really, that it took so long for the Dutch to pay attention to that period.

*In 1968, so after the* Nul *group had disbanded, you had a solo exhibition at the Stedelijk Museum entitled* Jan Henderikse Uses Common Cents. *'Uses common sense' – is this still the spirit of* Nul *talking?*

I've always felt that as an artist you should use your common sense; that's not specifically *Nul.* Marcel Duchamp said it: 'bête comme un peintre', dumb as a painter. Artists shouldn't philosophize too much about their own work; it only leads to problems and nonsense. I've always felt an affinity with Duchamp, with the combination of doing serious work but not taking yourself too seriously. Duchamp was a master at self-contradiction, at stirring up tensions time and time again. You can see this in his work: every step is a surprise. Wim Beeren, the director of the Stedelijk Museum in the 1980s, said this about my work too, that I'm so unpredictable. Make what you enjoy, whether it fits in a particular pattern or not. A lot of artists just go on doing things in the same familiar way. Sort of 'don't rock the boat', don't change too much, because it might all go wrong. To me that's death. I've never wanted to conform; I wouldn't even be able to. What Wim Beeren meant is that people expect an assemblage from me, but instead they get the Dutch national anthem, as *my* work of art, or an installation of cola bottles. That infuriates people. Because they don't get it – it runs counter to their expectations.

*You've mentioned Marcel Duchamp.*
*What are your thoughts on the conceptual element in your own work?*

I've always believed that art is really more an idea than a thing. I think. I once had an exhibition in mind in which I wouldn't make any of the pieces myself, and I wouldn't even go to see it. Maybe that's going too far; it would be *too* consistent. My installations of fruit boxes and beer crates from 1962 are of course the original pieces. But the point is the idea, not that one initial version. Forget the patina, forget the old signature, forget the original work; the value of the later versions of the installations lies somewhere amidst all that, and they are really just as unique as the original version. I was already working with fruit and vegetable boxes and beer crates in 1959, and I also made my first large installations in my studio that year. I only showed them in 1962, first at the Stedelijk Museum and later at the Antwerp exhibition *Anti-Peinture*. Yes, when you look back the idea turns out to be stronger than that one execution in and of itself.

*You talked earlier about a shared way of thinking.*
*And yet you didn't take part in the second* Nul *exhibition*
*in Amsterdam in 1965*

That's right. In fact I dropped out in 1964, because I didn't take part in the *Nul/ZERO* exhibition at the Gemeente Museum in The Hague in 1964. Jan Schoonhoven and I did exchange letters about that show, but I was already over it by then. It had all got a little too serious, too white, too clean and '*ZERO*ist'. In the early years it was different; the Dutch artists had a clear identity of their own, averse to idealism. Very different from the Germans, both feet more on the ground, really. It got a little too 'rein und hoch' for me. I still sent in a proposal for *ZERO on Sea* in 1966, because the idea of art in public space has always appealed to me enormously. When I think back, you can see a definite difference from the German

*ZERO* group, from those light pieces by Otto Piene, for instance. I'd done a design for a room built out of beer crates, with a light bulb inside each beer bottle. And then those light bulbs would flash on and off like mad, preferably at random, of course, not all at the same time. I've always loved quantities, masses, preferably of everyday objects. It's provocative but it's also beautiful, the way the packed stands of a baseball field are beautiful. It's decoration in the classical sense of the term, even though it's to do with things that others might find banal. Unlike many other artists, by the way, I don't think 'decoration' is a dirty word!

*Arman also worked with everyday objects and materials. How did your work from the* Nul *period relate to Arman's?*

I saw Arman's *Poubelles* for the first time in Paris; those pieces made a huge impression on me. Stuffing the contents of a rubbish bin inside a Plexiglas box – you couldn't get any more radical than that, I thought. I was also working with anything I came across, but I had the feeling that there was more of a 'choice' in my work than in Arman's. Making art without technique, totally devoid of any technique at all – I admired that enormously, although Arman's work was often much more composed than mine. And just recently I heard that he was in fact quite selective before those Plexiglas boxes of rubbish were sealed. I never say anything about my own work; for that you'll have to go to art historians. Still I think my work is more intuitive, less constructed. Arman, myself, but also Christo, Armando and of course Daniel Spoerri, so many people in those days were looking for 'it' in ordinary things, and yet each found it in his own way. Günther Uecker once asked me very politely whether he might make a piece with corks, just as I was doing a lot back then. But of course that piece looked completely different from mine, really composed, laid out in rows – I'd never do it that way. The Korean artist Nam June Paik once said that television had been such a new and dramatic form of entertainment that it allowed artists to go back to making dull and repetitive work. Maybe that's not such a crazy notion. My favourite things to work with are ordinary things,

things others find totally uninteresting or fail to notice entirely. Discarded photos, corks, coins, number plates, you name it. When I look back on it, that really is a constant line in my work, right up to the present day, in fact. And then all those ordinary things suddenly turn out to be very interesting indeed. I've said it many times before: I'm interested in everything that moves human beings. *Everything*. Preferably in large quantities. The more the merrier, too much is not enough! To me that really sums it up best.

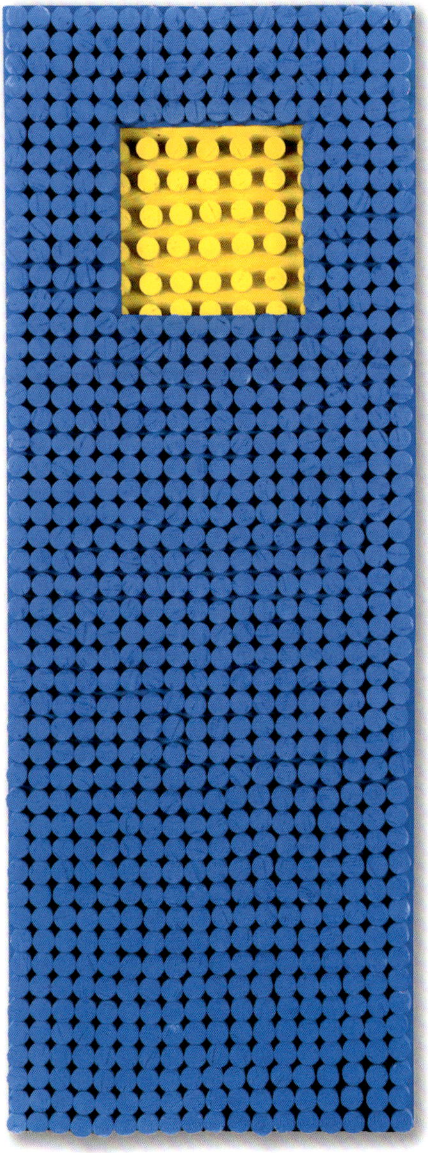

*Untitled*, 1968

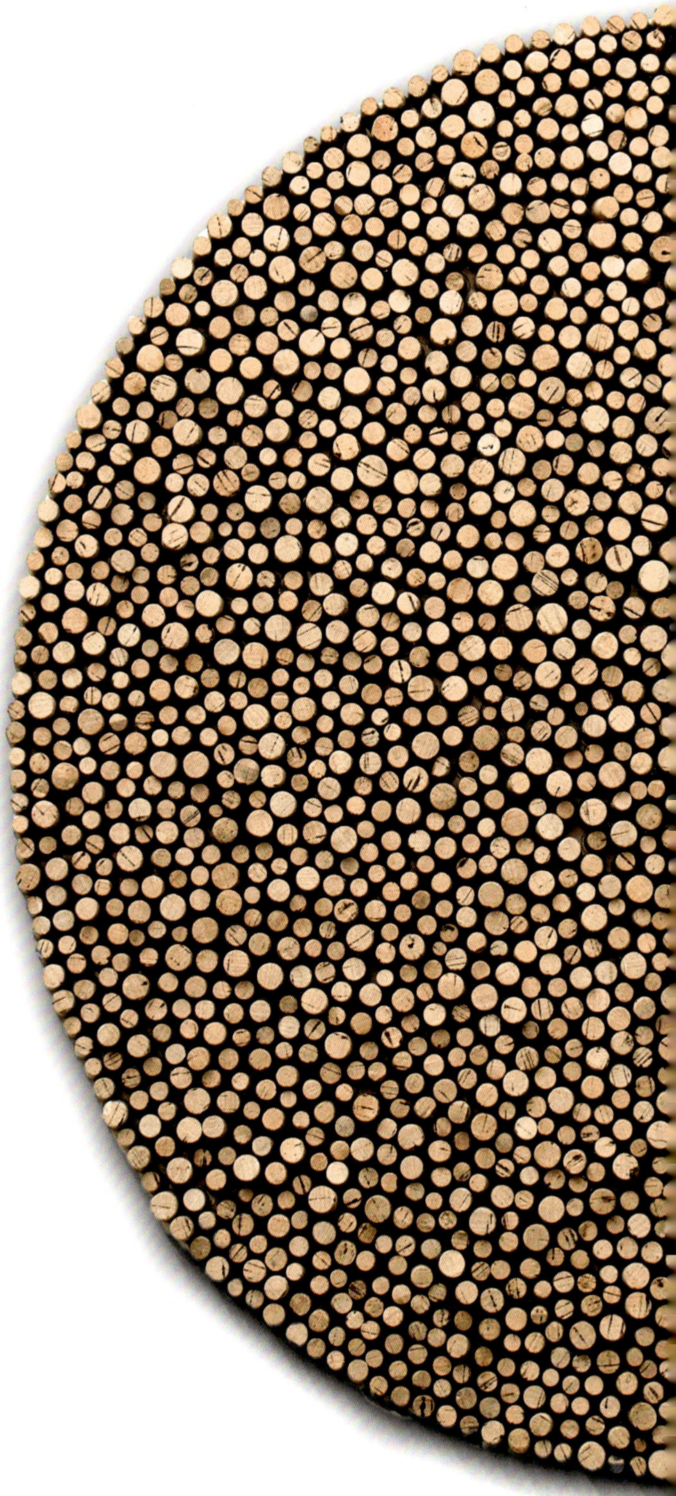

*Round, 2017*

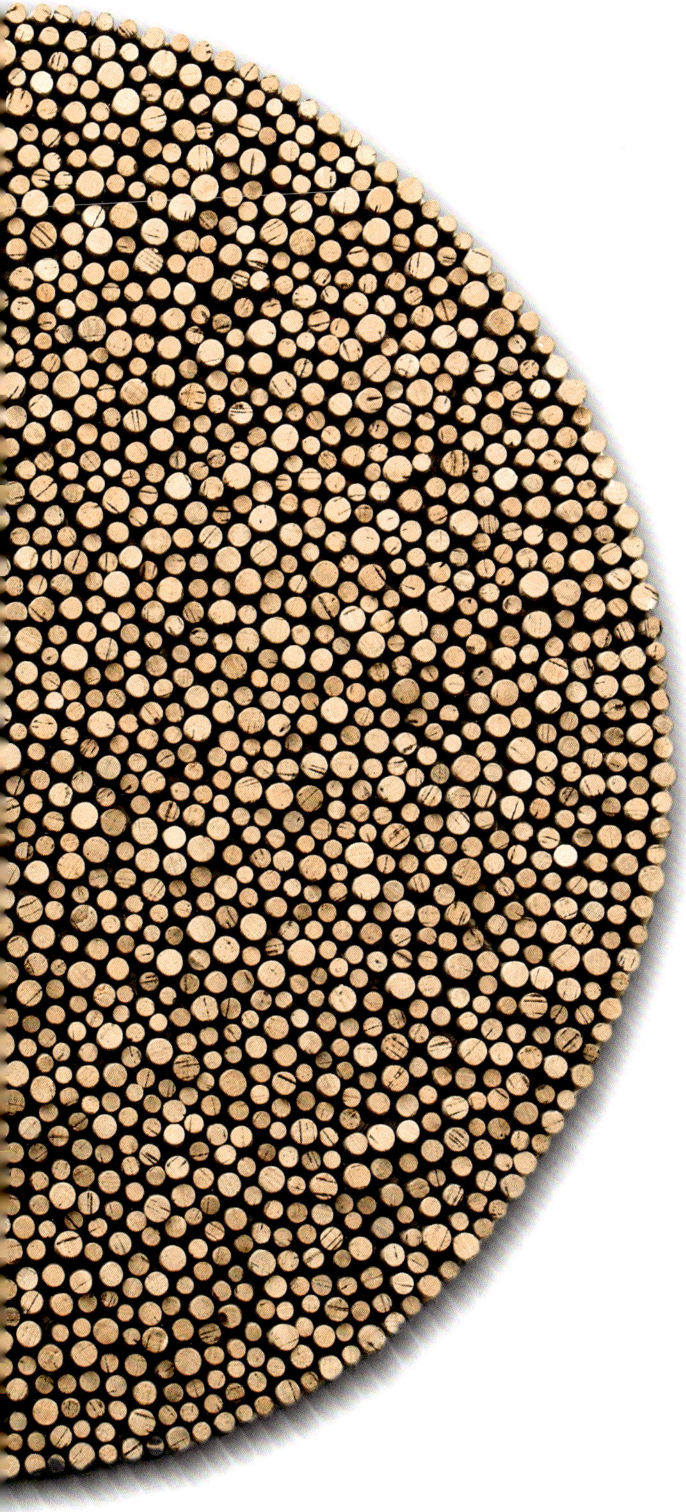

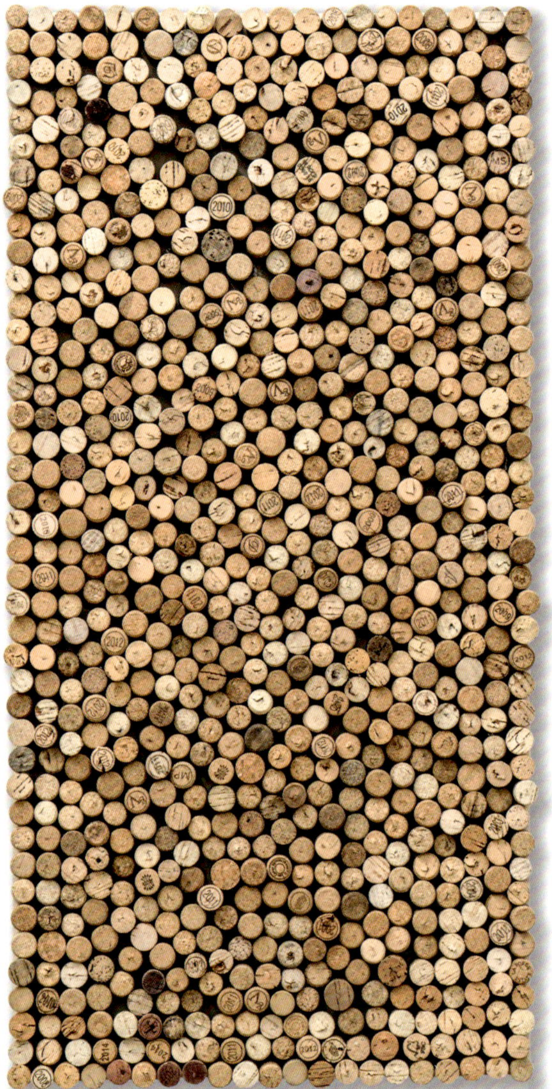

*Top*, 2016

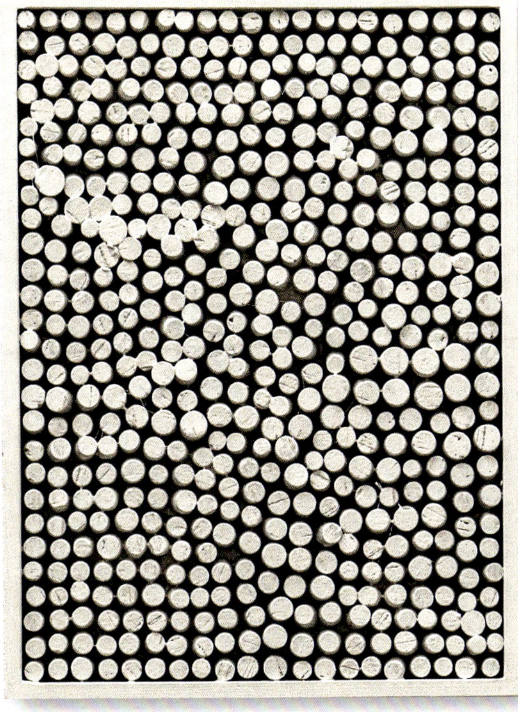

*Much*, 2017

*MAT*, 2016

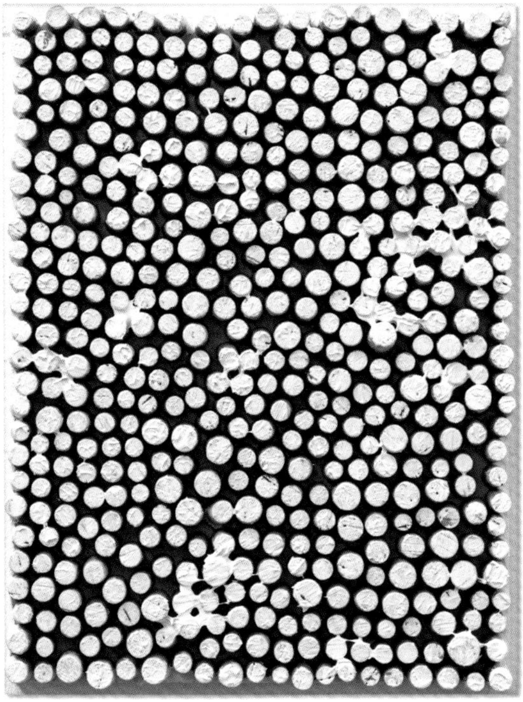

*Pearls*, 2016

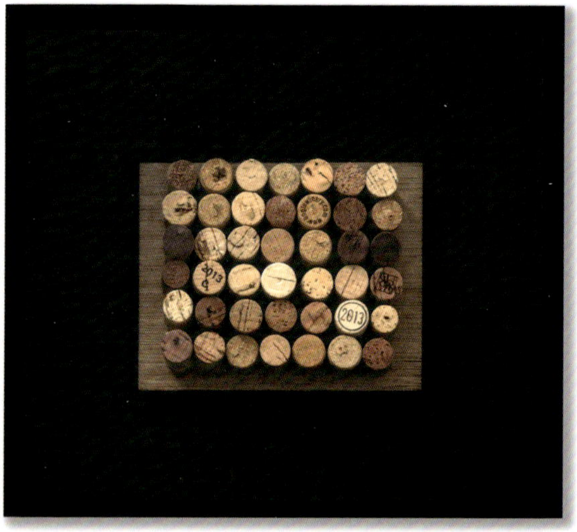

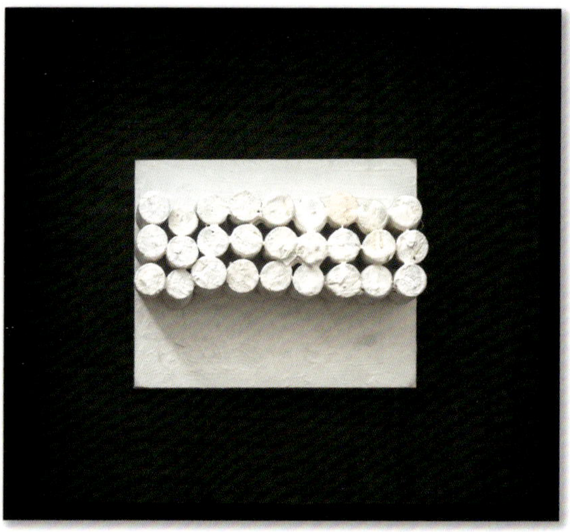

*Untitled*, 2014 | *Untitled*, 2014

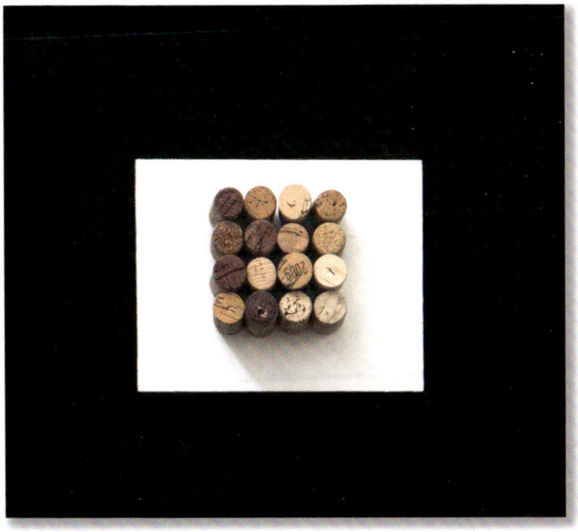

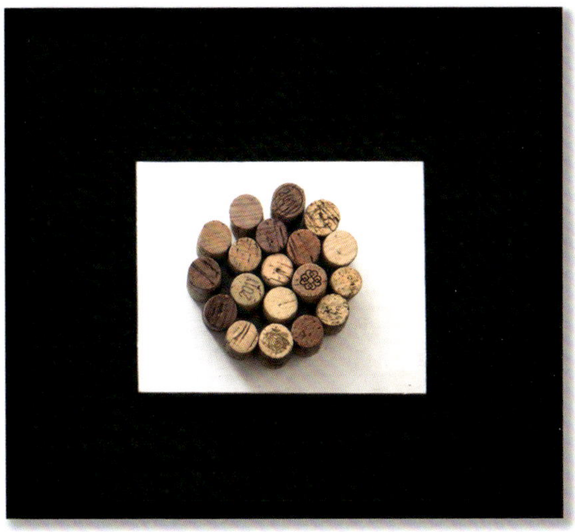

*Untitled*, 2014 | *Untitled*, 2014

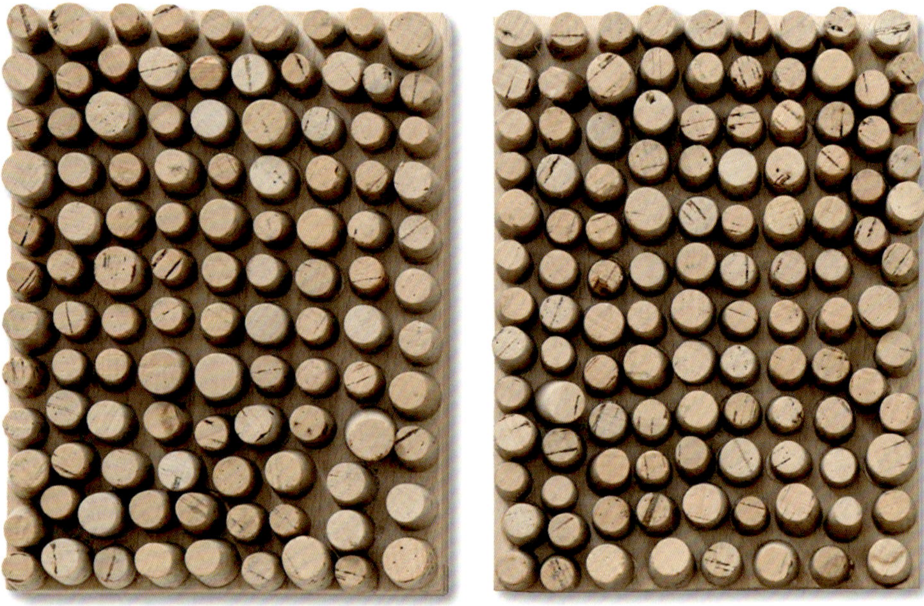

Natuur I - II - III – IV, 2016

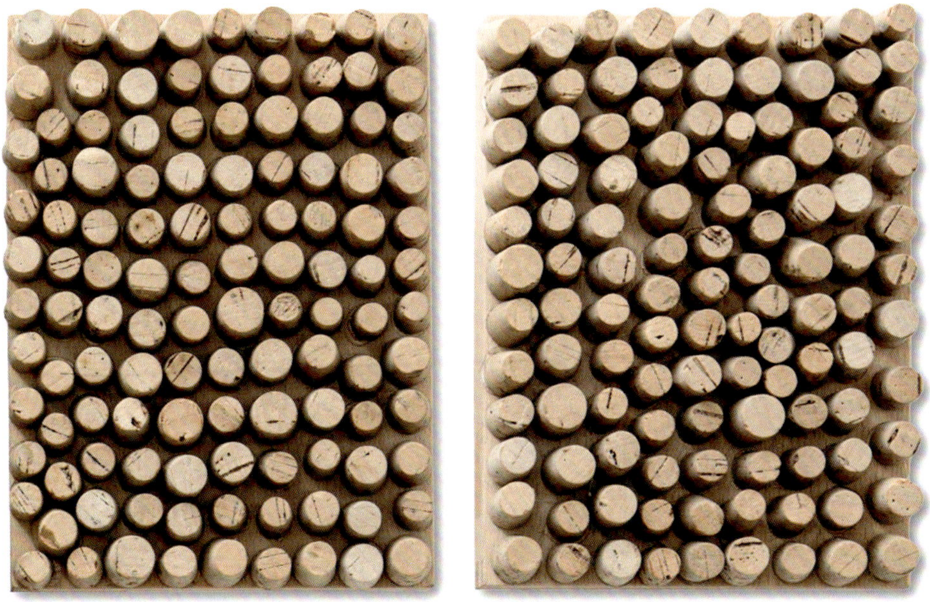

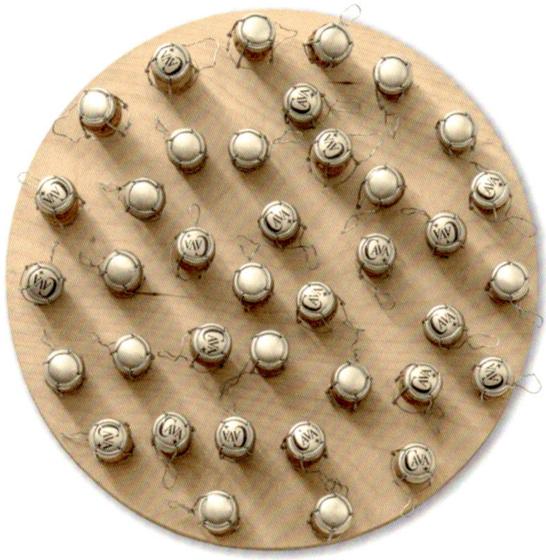

*Hoedjes*, 2015

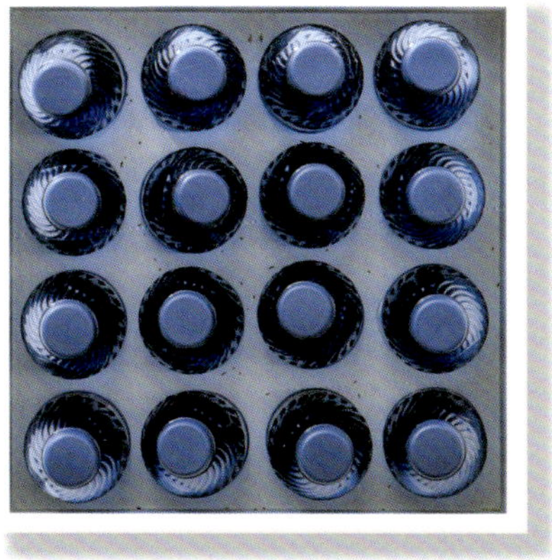

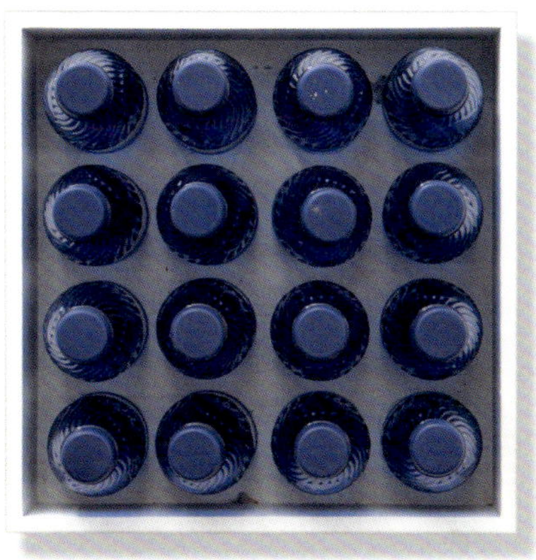

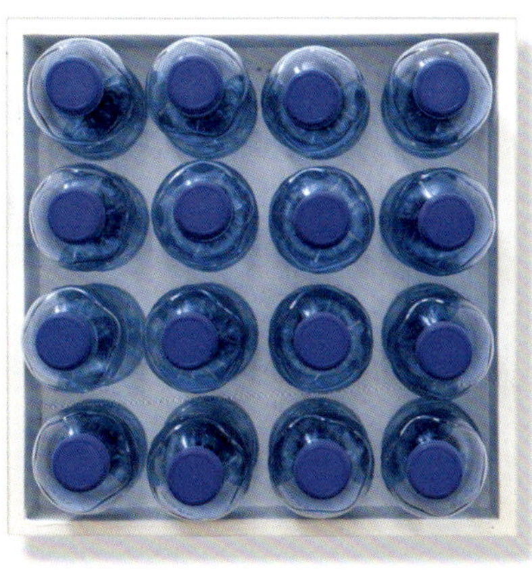

*Blue*, 2017 | *Blu*, 2017 | *Reine*, 2017

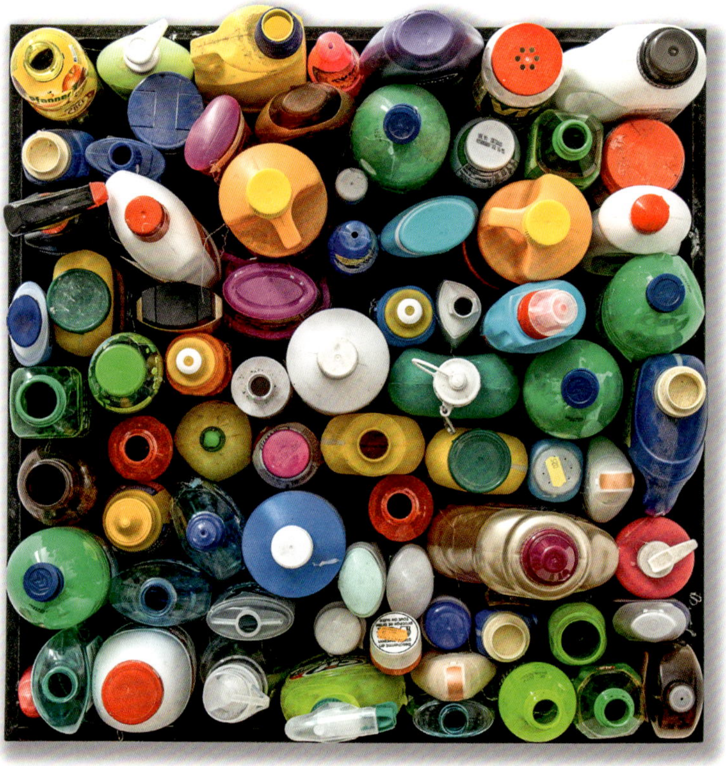

*Plastic Bottles*, 2016

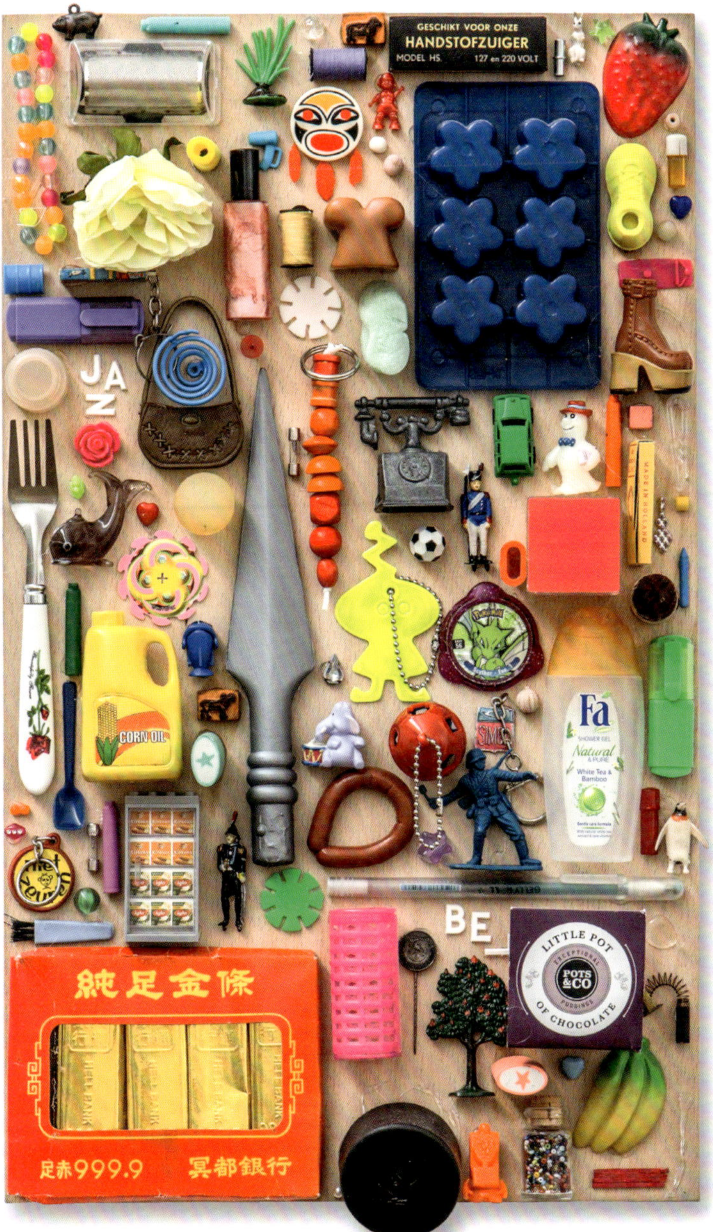
GESCHIKT VOOR ONZE
HANDSTOFZUIGER
MODEL HS. 127 en 220 VOLT
CORN OIL
Fa
SHOWER GEL
Natural & PURE
White Tea & Bamboo
BE
LITTLE POT
POTS &CO
OF CHOCOLATE
純足金條
足赤999.9
冥都銀行

999.9, 2016

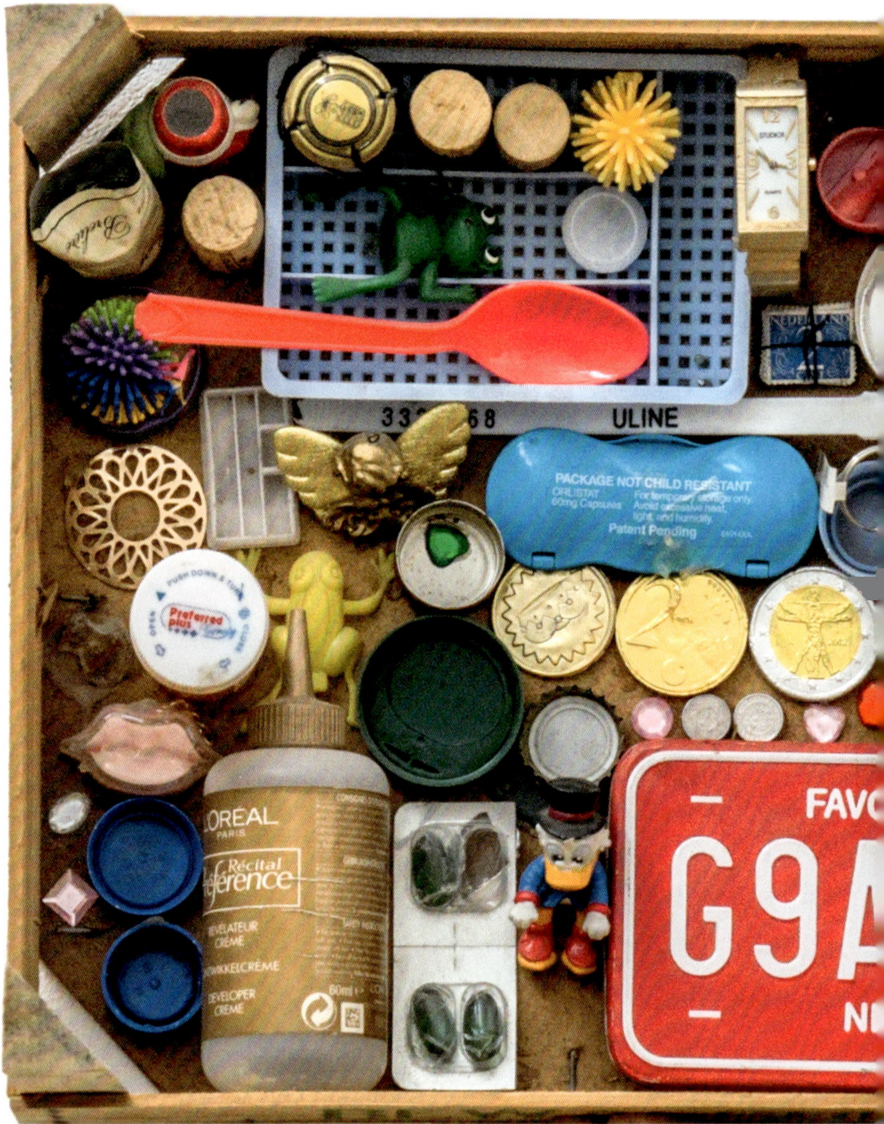


*Untitled*, 2015

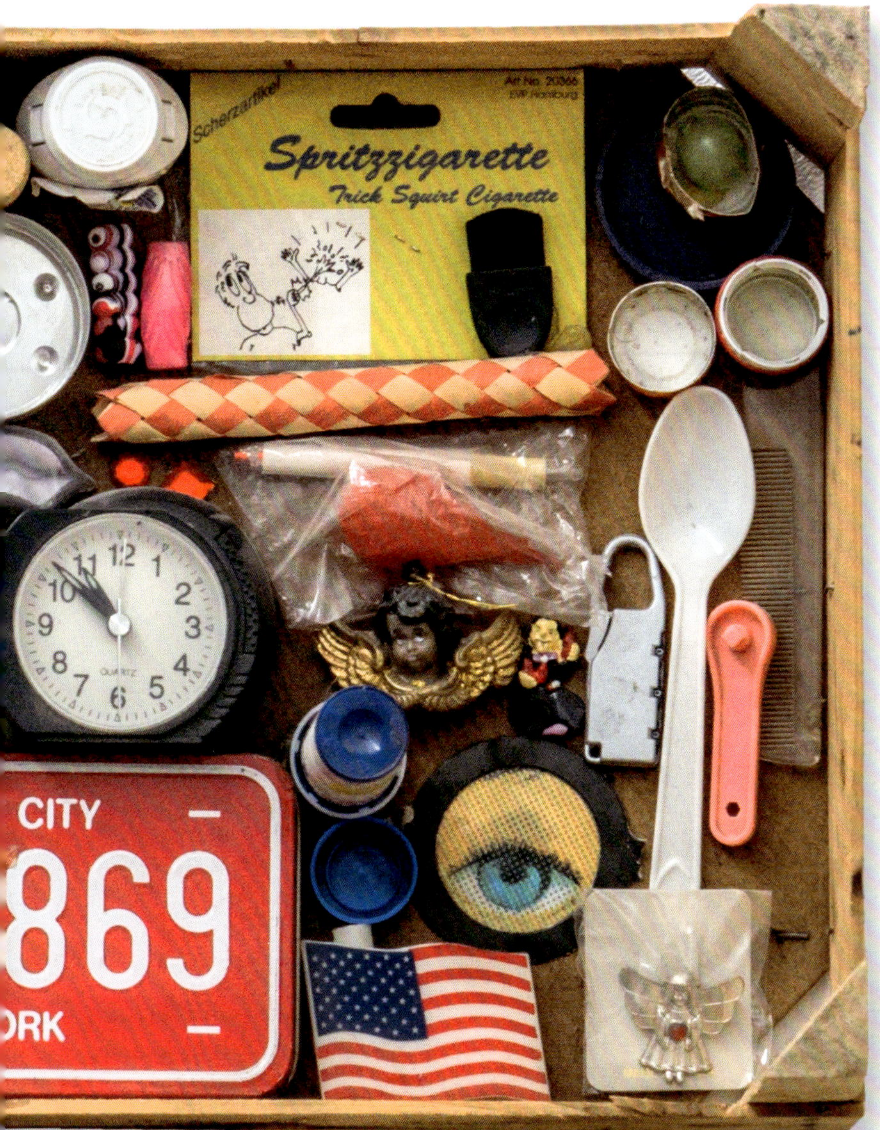
Scherzartikel
Spritzzigarette
Trick Squirt Cigarette
CITY
869
ORK

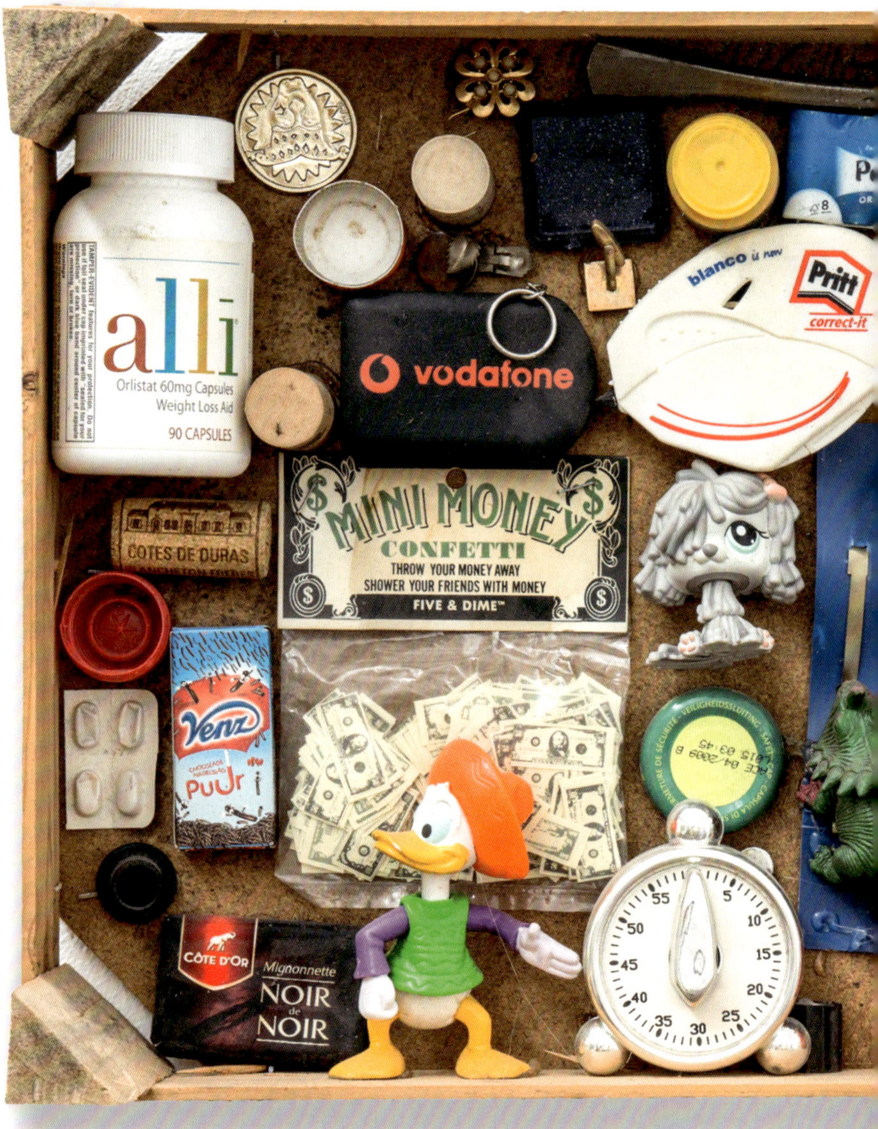


*Untitled*, 2011

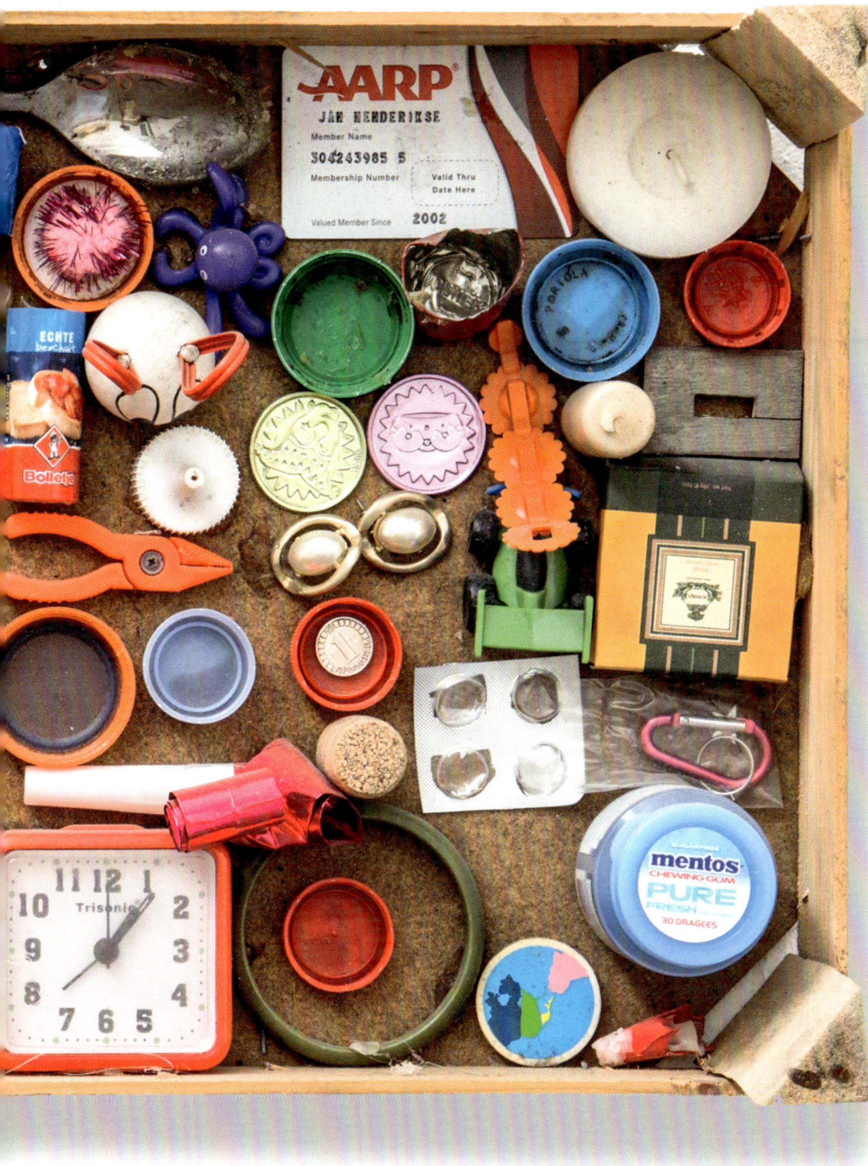
AARP
JAN HENDERIKSE
Member Name
304243985 5
Membership Number
Valid Thru
Date Here
Valued Member Since 2002
ECHTE
beschuit
Bolletje
mentos
CHEWING GUM
PURE
FRESH
30 DRAGEES

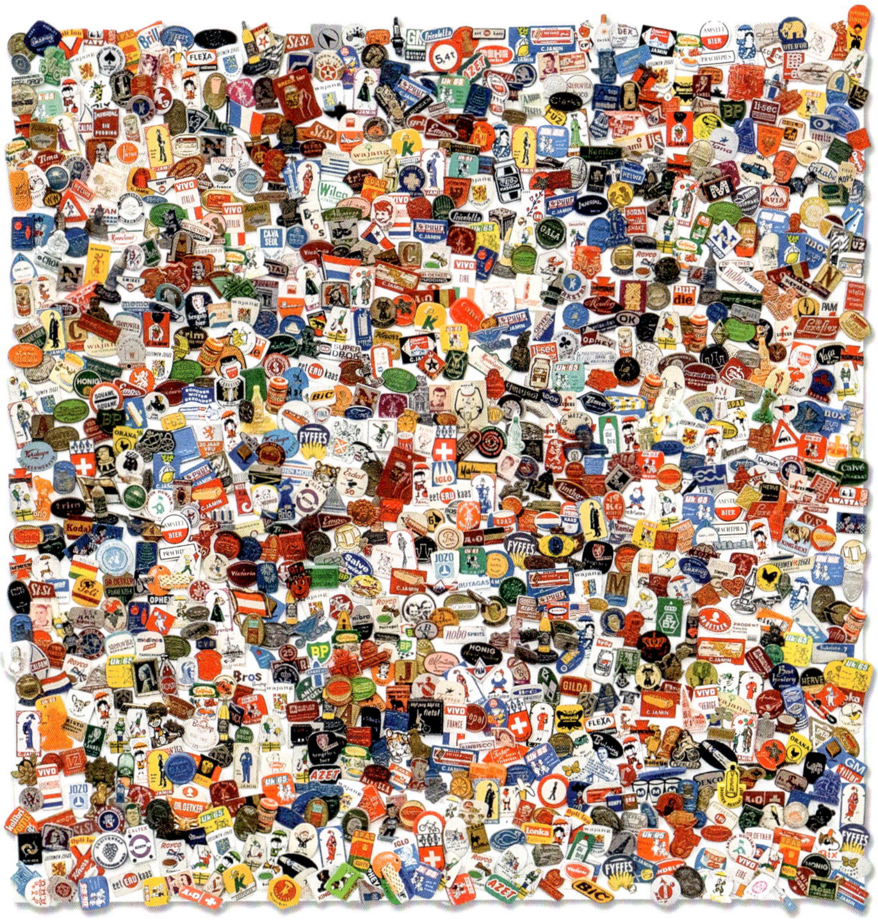

Speldjes, 2016

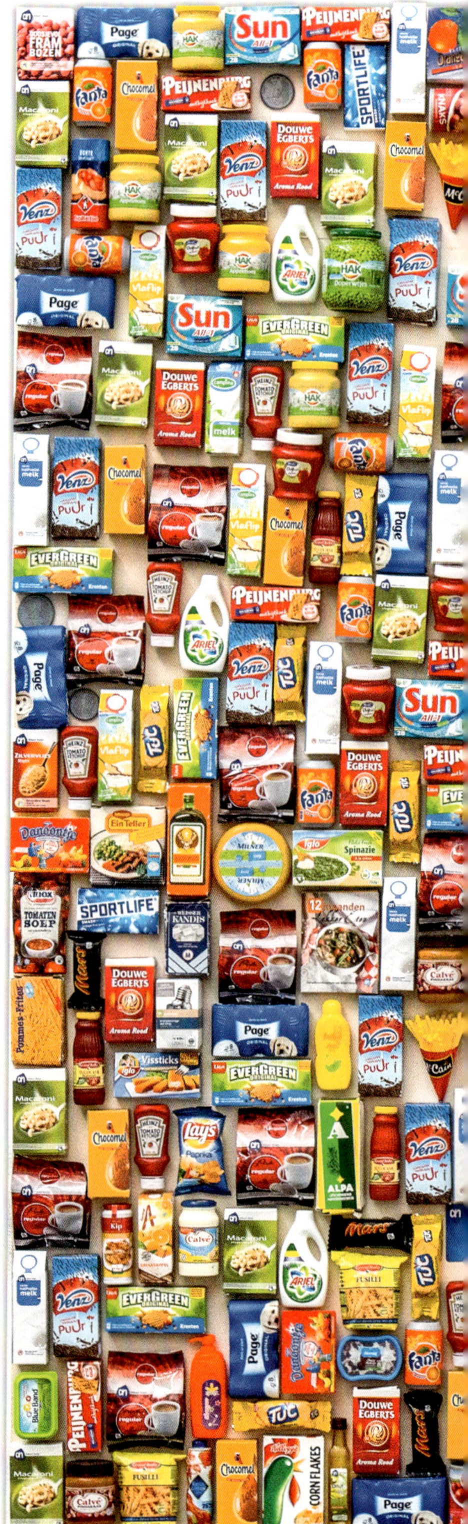
Sun
Page
Peijnenburg
Fanta
Sportlife
Chocomel
Venz
Douwe Egberts
Macaroni
HAK
Ariel
Evergreen
Vla Flip
TUC
Mars
Lays
Calvé
Corn Flakes
Fusilli
Spinazie
Vissticks
Ein Teller
Blue Band

De Boer, 2016

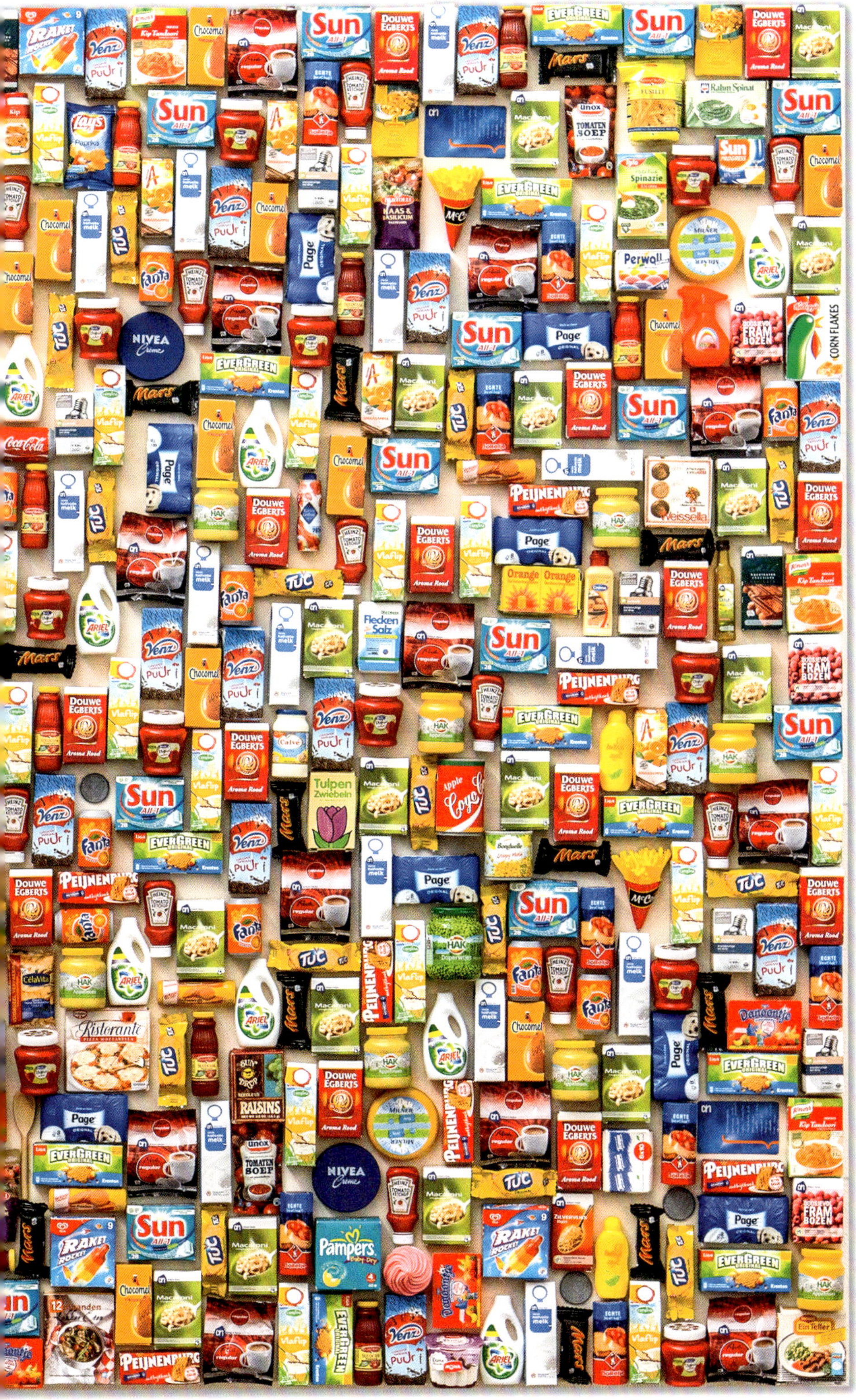

Sun
All-1
Douwe Egberts
Aroma Rood
Venz
Puur
Mars
Evergreen
Chocomel
Lay's
Paprika
Unox
Tomaten Soep
Fusilli
Rahm Spinat
Spinazie
Macaroni
Page
Tuc
Fanta
Nivea Creme
Perwoll
Ariel
Corn Flakes
Coca-Cola
Vla Flip
Peijnenburg
Weissella
Orange
HAK
Fleckensalz
Tulpen Zwiebeln
Apple
Raket
Rocket
Ristorante
CéLaVita
Raisins
Danoontje
Pampers
Ein Teller
Zilveruien
Knorr
Kip Tandoori
Frambozen
Egte

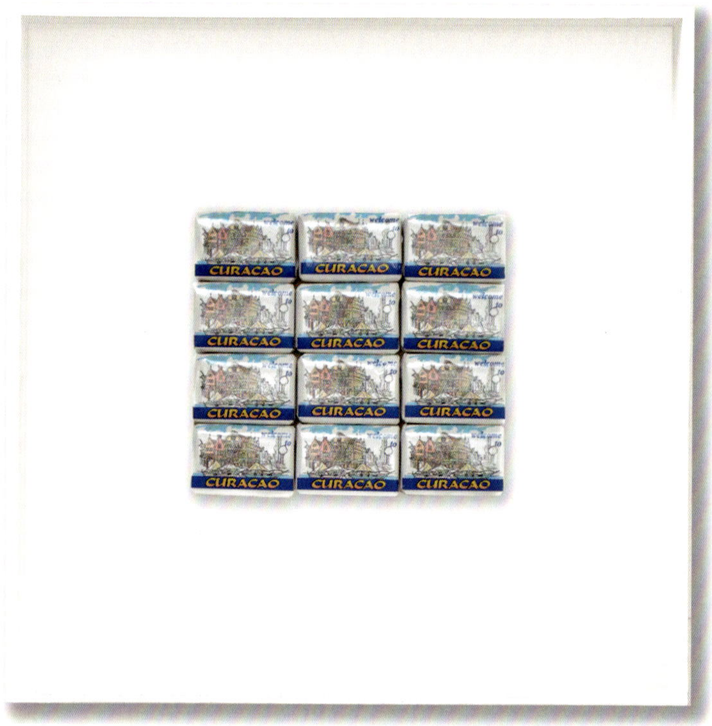


*Welcome*, 2005

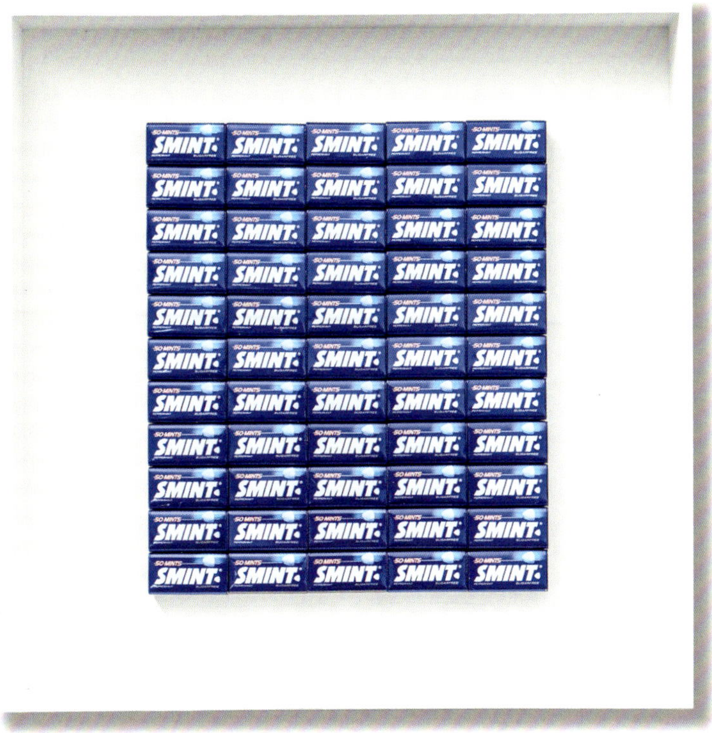


*Mint*, 2017

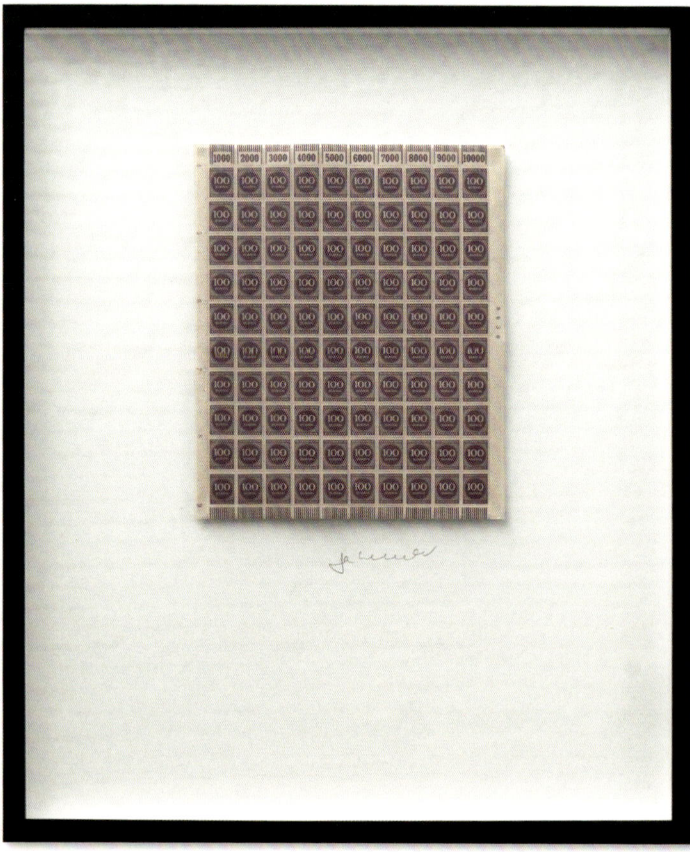

*100 Mark, 2016*

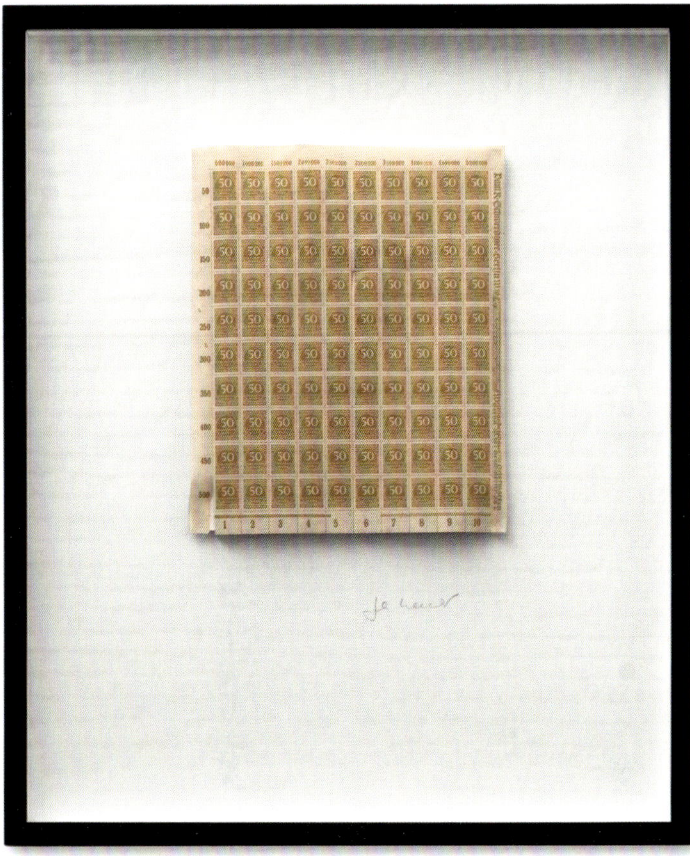

*RM 50.000, 2016*

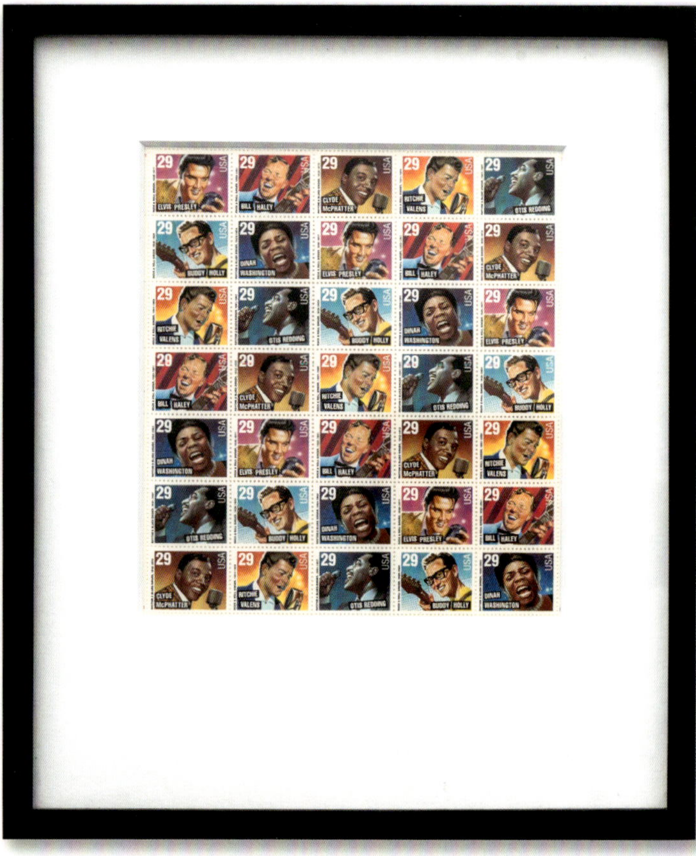

*I Am a Rock and Roll Man*, 1991

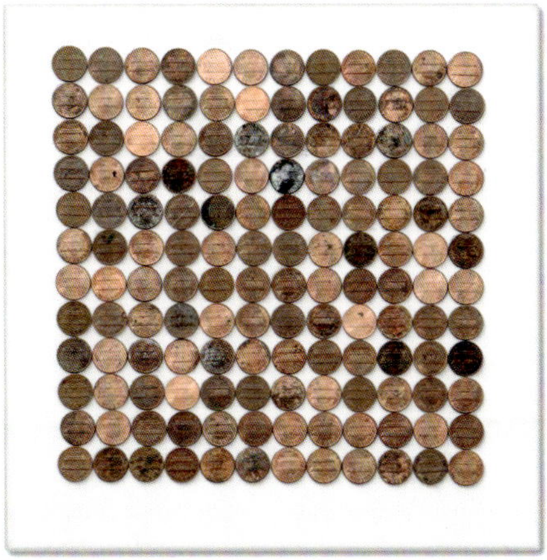

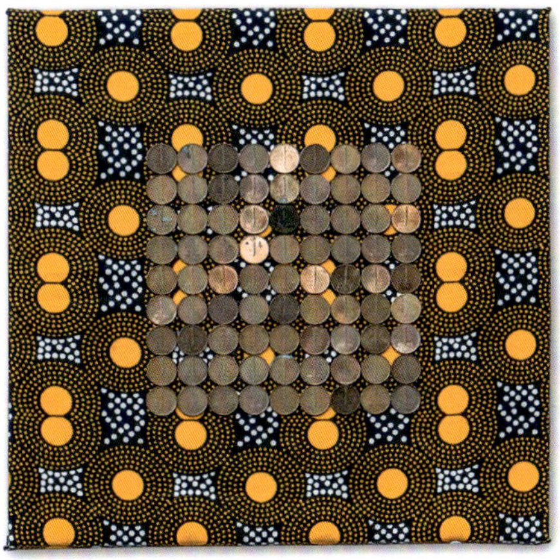

*1 Gross*, 2017 | *Untitled*, 2012

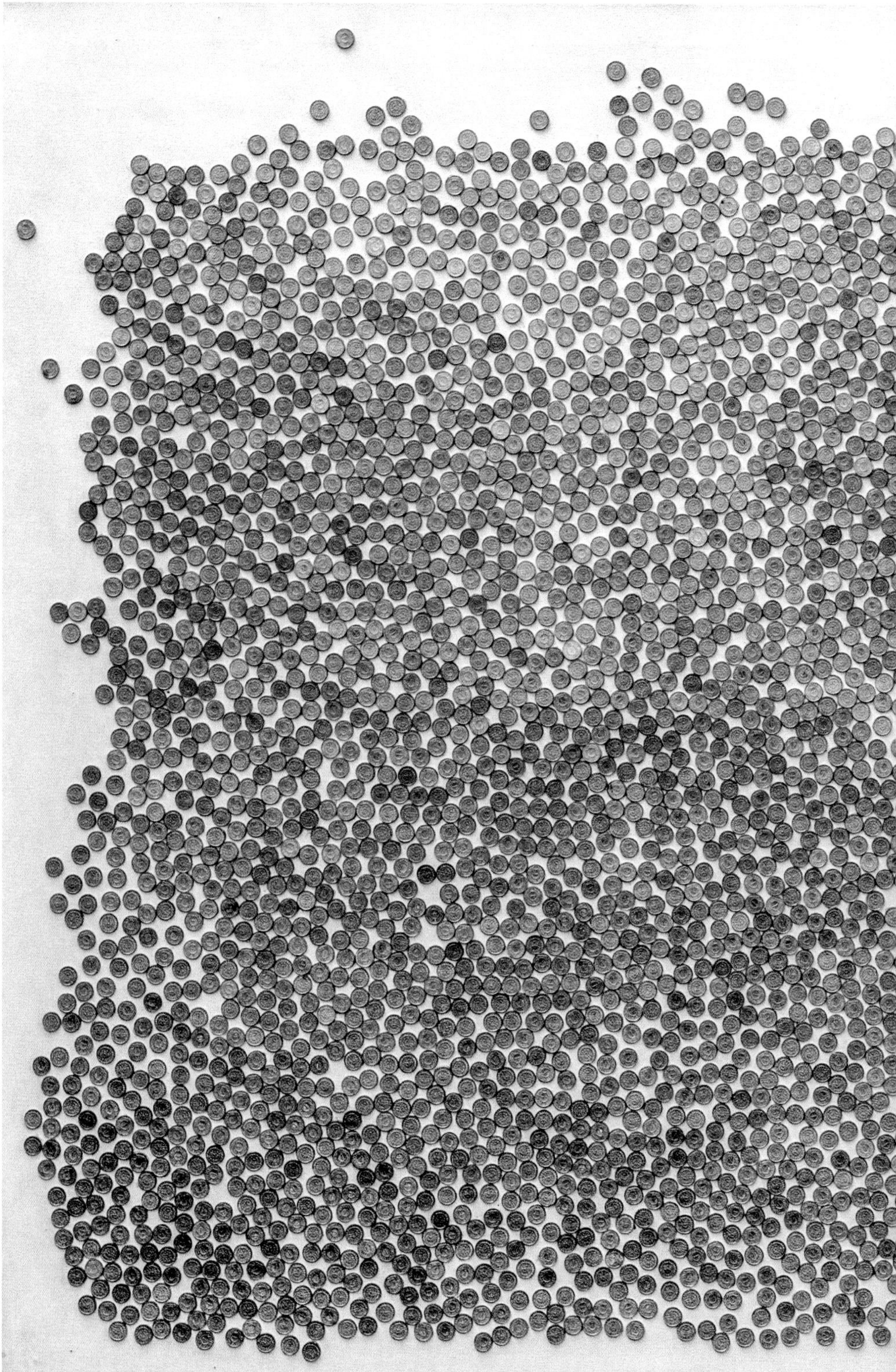

*The Full*, 2007

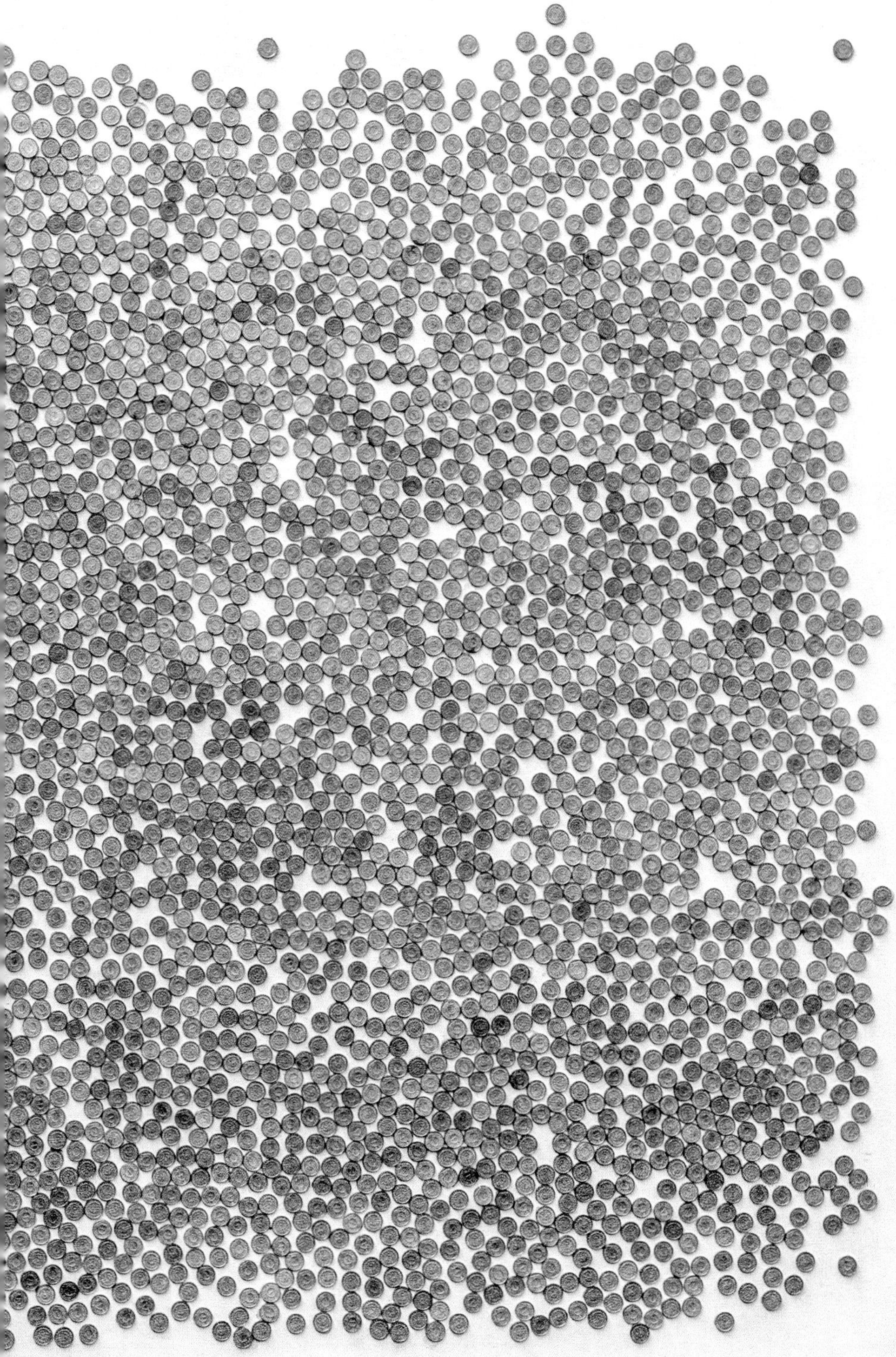

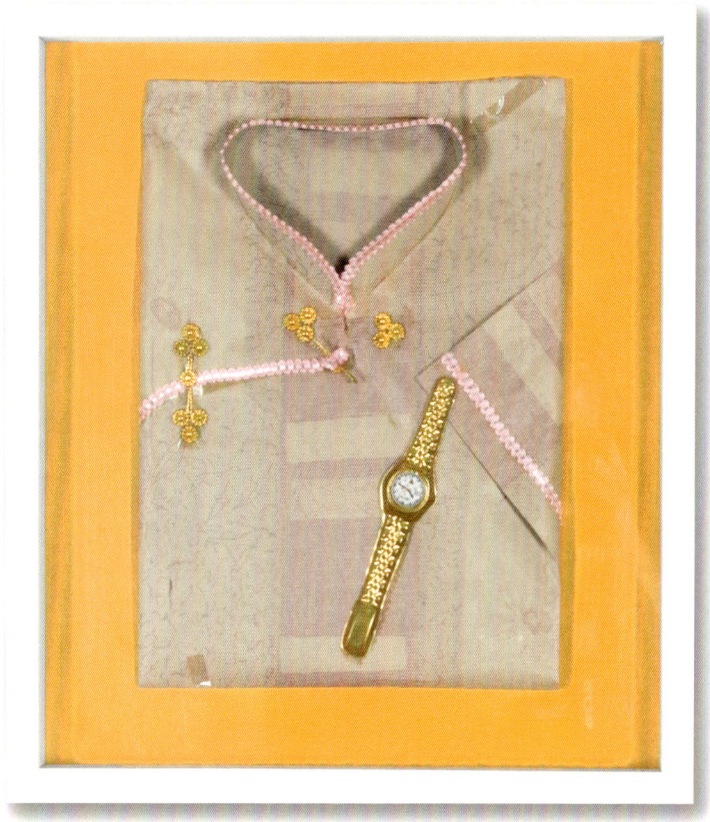

*Golden Watch*, 2005

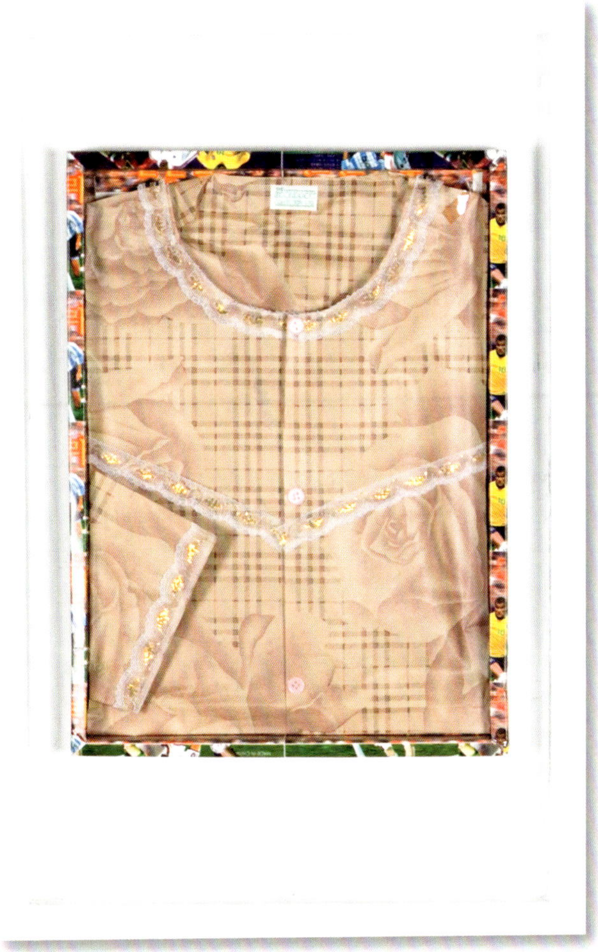

*Untitled*, 2006

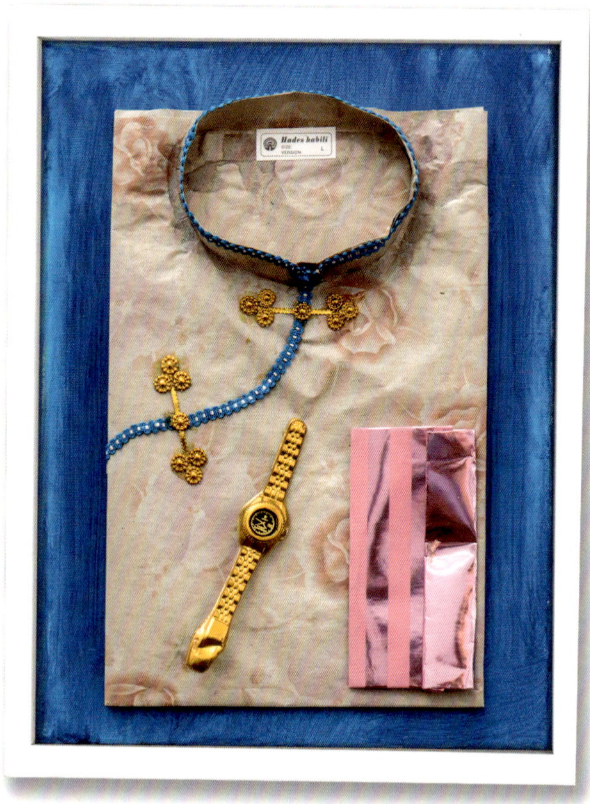


*Hades Habili*, 2006

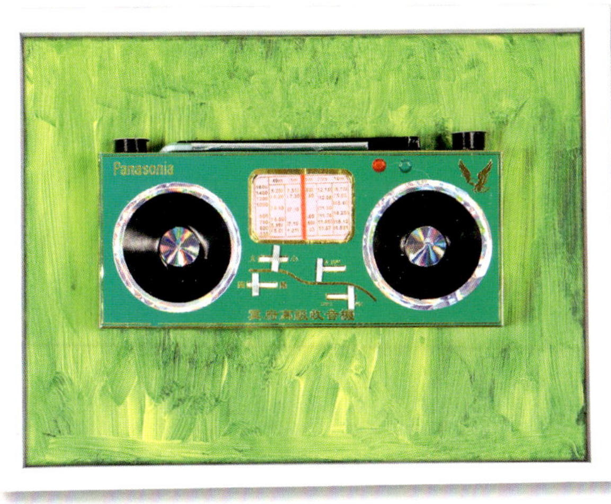


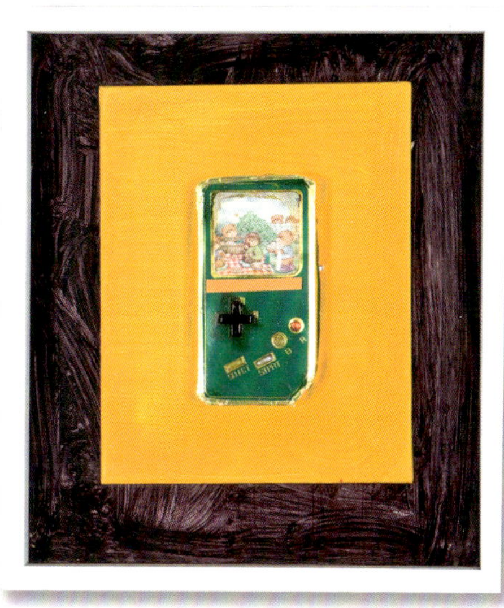

*Panasonia*, 2006 | *Smart*, 2007

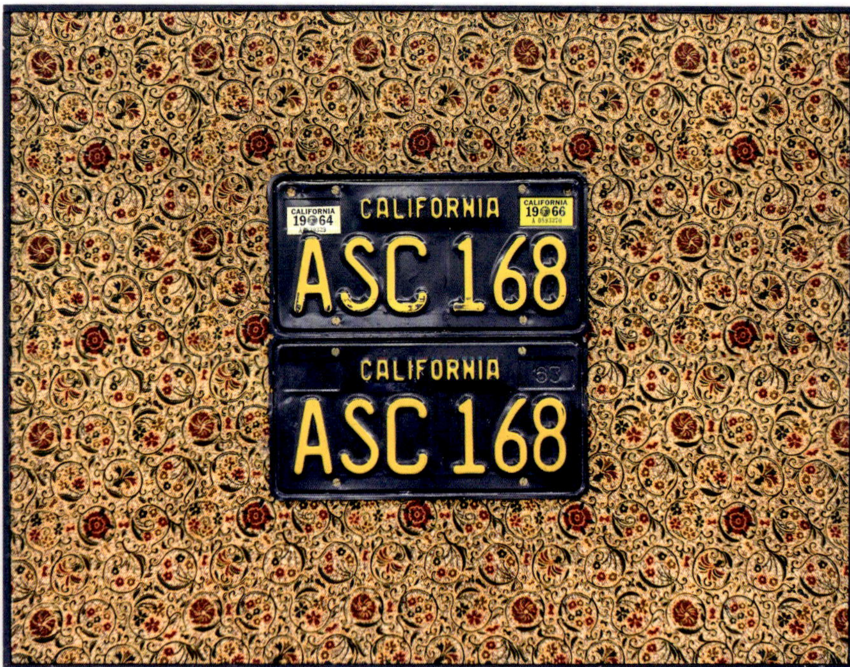
CALIFORNIA
1964
CALIFORNIA
CALIFORNIA
1966
ASC 168
CALIFORNIA
63
ASC 168

*PP 11 – A, 1966*

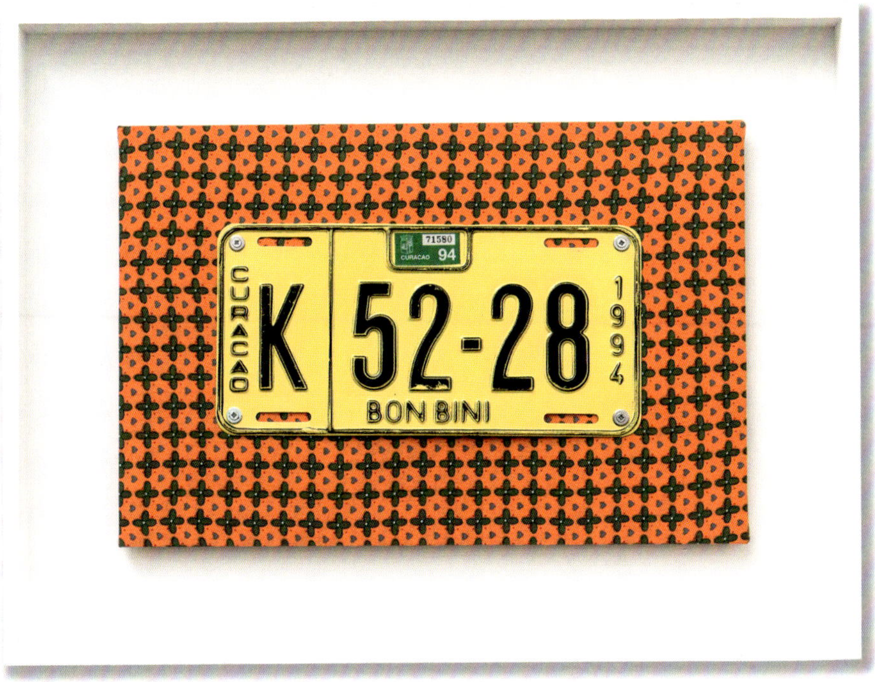


28, 2016

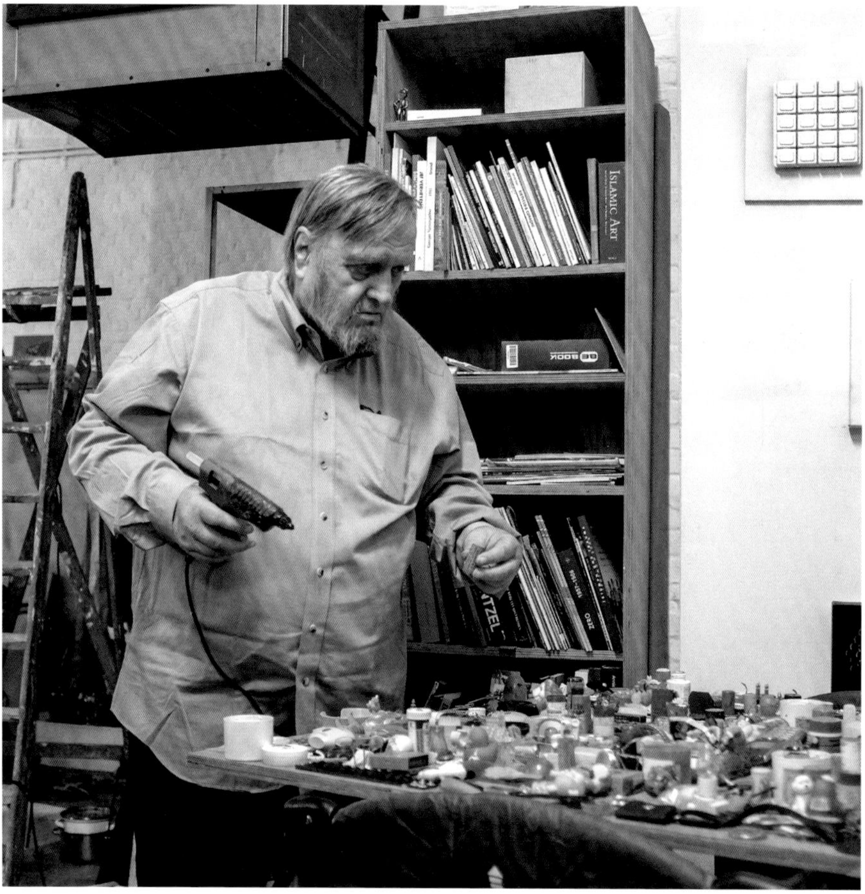


Foto | Photo: Robbert Fortgens, 2014

Der internationale Künstler **JAN HENDERIKSE** (geb. 1937 in Delft) studierte an der Freien Akademie in Den Haag und ist eine der Schlüsselfiguren der europäischen Kunst nach 1960. 1959 siedelte Henderikse um nach Köln, kurz danach nach Düsseldorf. Während seiner Zeit in Düsseldorf, eines der Epizentren der europäischen Nachkriegsavantgarde, kam Henderikse in Kontakt mit dem Kreis der internationalen *ZERO*-Künstler, bewahrte dabei aber eine gewisse Unabhängigkeit. Im Nachhinein kann diese Periode als Reifeprozess betrachtet werden, als konzeptuelle Basis für die darauffolgenden Schaffensjahre des Künstlers.

Ab dem Moment, in dem er die Niederlande verließ, hat Henderikse nie wieder gemalt. Die Ufer des Rheins dienten ihm als Stätten reicher Ausbeute bei der Produktion seiner ersten Assemblagen: Holzkisten und –tafeln, in die er Treibgut, Flaschen, Kronenkorken und Ampullen einsetzte. 1961 formierte Henderikse gemeinsam mit Armando, Henk Peeters und Jan Schoonhoven die holländische Gruppe *Nul*, die an etlichen bedeutenden internationalen Ausstellungen teilnahm. Die Ausstellung *Nul* 1962 im Amsterdamer Stedelijk Museum präsentierte Henderikses Installation gestapelter Bierkisten, eine der ersten kommerziell unterstützten Kunstprojekte der Niederlande.

Henderikse lebte von 1963 bis 1967 in Curaçao und arbeitete dort mit gefundenen Gegenständen und Fotografien. Seine Assemblagen aus – für die damalige Zeit gewiss verwirrenden – Konglomeraten waren von einer großen Zufälligkeit der Materialauswahl geprägt. Die ersten Assemblagen mit Münzen entstanden 1965 und drücken die nachhaltige Faszination des Künstlers für Wiederholung, Masse und Komposition mittels einer Rasterstruktur aus.

Henderikse wechselte 1968 nach New York, demselben Jahr, in dem er 32 Münz-Reliefs in seiner Einzelausstellung *Jan Henderikse Uses Common Cents* im Amsterdamer Stedelijk Museum präsentierte. Im Zeitabschnitt von Mitte der 1970er bis Mitte der 1980er Jahre, einst von ihm als Ende der traditionellen Kunst charakterisiert – „keine Kunst mehr an den Wänden" – brachte Henderikse eine Menge von Filmmaterial hervor, das eine weitere Facette des Alltagslebens in der höchst markanten Bildsprache des

Künstlers darstellt. Ab den frühen 1980er Jahren publizierte Henderikse eine große Anzahl von Künstlerbüchern, die in signifikanten Archiven, Bibliotheken und Museumssammlungen weltweit enthalten sind.

Henderikse ging 1987/88 nach Berlin, wo er bis 2001 ein zweites Atelier unterhielt. Der Künstler lebt gegenwärtig in Brooklyn, New York, und in Antwerpen. Retrospektive Einzelausstellungen in Schwerin und in Kiel (2007) sowie Beiträge zu Gruppenausstellungen der jüngeren Zeit in Amsterdam, Berlin, Düsseldorf, Johannesburg, London, New York, Nizza und Tokio belegen das anhaltende und wachsende Interesse an Henderikses multimedialem Werk.

International artist **JAN HENDERIKSE** (Delft, 1937) studied at the Free Academy in The Hague and is one of the key players in European art after 1960. In 1959 Henderikse moved to Cologne, and shortly thereafter to Düsseldorf. While in Düsseldorf, one of the epicentres of the post-war European avant-garde, Henderikse made contact with the circle of international *ZERO* artists, though maintaining a certain degree of independence. In hindsight, these years can be considered as a 'coming of age', as a conceptual basis for the years that followed.

Since the moment he left the Netherlands, Henderikse has never painted again. With the banks of the Rhine as his foraging grounds he created his first assemblages; wooden crates and panels filled with flotsam, plastic bottles, crown caps, and ampoules. In 1961, together with Armando, Henk Peeters and Jan Schoonhoven, Henderikse formed the Dutch *Nul* Group, which took part in several major international exhibitions. The exhibition *Nul* at the Amsterdam Stedelijk Museum in 1962, showed Henderikse's installation of stacked beer crates, one of the first commercially sponsored art project of the Netherlands.

Henderikse settled in Curaçao from 1963-67, working with found objects and photographs. His assemblages are, certainly for that time, perplexing amalgamations with a large degree of randomness regarding the choice of material. The first assemblages with coins originate from 1965 and are expressions of a recurring fascination for repetition, multitude and composition by means of a grid.

Henderikse moved to New York in 1968, the same year in which he showed 32 coin reliefs in his solo exhibition *Jan Henderikse Uses Common Cents* in the Amsterdam Stedelijk Museum.The period from the mid-seventies to mid-eighties, once characterized by Henderikse as the end of traditional art – "no more art on the wall" – yielded a large amount of film material, portraying yet another slice of everyday life in Henderikse's highly distinctive vocabulary. From the early eighties on, Henderikse published a vast number of artist's books, many of which are included in major archives, libraries and museum collections worldwide.

Henderikse moved to Berlin in 1987-88 and kept a second studio there until 2001. The artist currently lives in Brooklyn, New York and Antwerp.

Retrospective solo exhibitions in Schwerin and Kiel (2007), and recent contributions to group exhibitions in Amsterdam, Berlin, Dusseldorf, Johannesburg, London, New York, Nice and Tokyo, reflect the ongoing and mounting interest in Henderikse's multimedia oeuvre.

Seite | *Page*

4 *Giesskanne*, 1987, 63,5 × 53 cm
Ready Made: Gummi-Objekt
*Rubber-object*

14 *Untitled*, 1968, 122 × 122 cm
Assemblage: Münzen auf Holzplatte
*Coins on panel*

23 *Untitled*, 1968, 122 × 45,5 × 10,5 cm
Assemblage: Korken auf Holzplatte, bemalt
*Painted corks on panel*

24-25 *Round*, 2017, 122 × 122 cm
Assemblage: Korken auf Holzplatte
*Corks on panel*

26 *Top*, 2016, 92 × 46 cm
Assemblage: Korken auf Holzplatte
*Corks on panel*

27 *Much*, 2017, 40 × 30 cm
Assemblage: Korken auf Holzplatte, bemalt
*Painted corks on panel*

28 *MAT*, 2016, 40 × 30 cm
Assemblage: Korken auf Holzplatte, bemalt
*Painted corks on panel*

29 *Pearls*, 2016, 40 × 30 cm
Assemblage: Korken auf Holzplatte, bemalt
*Painted corks on panel*

30 *Untitled*, 2014, 32 × 37 cm
Assemblage: Korken auf Holzplatte
*Corks on panel*

*Untitled*, 2014, 32 × 37 cm
Assemblage: Korken auf Holzplatte, bemalt
*Painted corks on panel*

31 *Untitled*, 2014, 27 × 37 cm
Assemblage: Korken auf Holzplatte
*Corks on panel*

*Untitled*, 2014, 27 × 37 cm
Assemblage: Korken auf Holzplatte
*Corks on panel*

32-33 *Natuur I - II - III – IV*, 2016, je | *each* 20 × 15 cm
Assemblage: Korken auf Holzplatte
*Corks on panel*

34 *Hoedjes*, 2015, 40 × 40 × 8 cm
Assemblage: Champagnerkorken auf Holzplatte
*Champagne corks on panel*

35 *Blue*, 2017, 30 × 30 cm
Assemblage: Plastikflaschen in Box
*Plastic bottles in box*

*Blu*, 2017, 30 × 30 cm
Assemblage: Plastikflaschen in Box
*Plastic bottles in box*

*Reine*, 2017, 30 × 30 cm
Assemblage: Plastikflaschen in Box
*Plastic bottles in box*

36 *Plastic Bottles*, 2016, 61 × 61 cm
Assemblage: Platikflaschen auf Holzplatte
*Plastic bottles on panel*

37 *999.9*, 2016, 50 × 30 cm
Bricolage auf Holzplatte
*Bricolage on panel*

38-39 *Untitled*, 2015, 29,5 × 50 cm
Bricolage in Holzkiste
*Bricolage in wooden crate*

40-41 *Untitled*, 2011, 29,50 × 50 cm
Bricolage in Holzkiste
*Bricolage in wooden crate*

43 *Speldjes*, 2016, 65,5 × 65,5 cm
Assemblage: Pins auf Leinwand
*Pins on canvas*

44-45 *De Boer*, 2016, 92 × 92 cm
Bricolage auf Holzplatte
*Bricolage on panel*

46 *Welcome*, 2005, 47,5 × 47,5 cm
Assemblage: Seifen auf Holzplatte
*Soaps on panel*

47 *Mint*, 2017, 65,5 × 65,5 cm
Assemblage: Metallboxen auf Holzplatte
*Metal boxes on panel*

48 *100 Mark*, 2016, 62,5 × 52,5 cm
Ready Made: Briefmarken
*Stamps*

49 *RM 50.000*, 2016, 62,5 × 52,5 cm
Ready Made: Briefmarken
*Stamps*

50 *I Am a Rock and Roll Man*, 1991, 40 × 33,5 cm
Ready Made: Briefmarken
*Stamps*

51 *Untitled*, 2012, 30 × 30 cm
Assemblage: Münzen und Stoff auf Holzplatte
*Coins and fabric on panel*

*1 Gross*, 2017, 30 × 30 cm
Assemblage: Münzen auf Leinwand
*Coins and on canvas*

52-53 *The Full*, 2007, 100 × 140 cm
Assemblage: Münzen auf Leinwand
*Coins and on canvas*

54 *Golden Watch*, 2005, 44 × 38,5 cm
Ready Made: Papierobjekt auf Leinwand
*Paper object on canvas*

55 *Untitled*, 2006, 64 × 54 cm
Ready Made: Papierobjekt auf Leinwand
*Paper object on canvas*

56 *Hades Habili*, 2006, 40 × 30 cm
Ready Made: Papierobjekt auf Leinwand
*Paper object on canvas*

57 *Panasonia*, 2006, 30 × 40 cm
Ready Made: Papierobjekt auf Leinwand
*Paper object on canvas*

*Smart*, 2007, 44 × 38,5 cm
Ready Made: Papierobjekt auf Leinwand
*Paper object on canvas*

58 *PP 11 – A*, 1966, 60 × 80 cm
Assemblage: Nummernschild und Stoff auf Holzplatte
*License plates and fabric on plate*

59 *28*, 2016, 46,5 × 62 cm
Assemblage: Nummernschild und Stoff auf Holzplatte
*License plates and fabric on plate*

2017 LEVY Galerie, Hamburg
Zaloudek Galerie, Prag | Prague
2016 Galerie Andrea Madesta, Regensburg
St. Petri Kultur- und Universitätskirche, Lübeck
*Kunst in Europa 1945-968*, ZKM | Zentrum für Kunst und Medientechnologie Karlsruhe, Karlsruhe (G)
2015 Galerie Schoots + Van Duyse, Antwerpen | Antwerp
Borzo Gallery, Amsterdam
*ZERO – Die internationale Kunstbewegung der 1950er und 1960er Jahre*, Martin-Gropius-Bau, Berlin (G)
*ZERO: Let us Explore the Stars*, Stedelijk Museum, Amsterdam (G)
2014 Galerie Schoots + Van Duyse, Antwerpen | Antwerp
*ZERO*: Countdown to Tomorrow, 1950s-60s, Solomon R. Guggenheim Museum, New York (G)
2013 K80 Galerie, Berlin
Galerie Schoots + Van Duyse, Antwerpen | Antwerp
2012 Borzo Modern & Contemporary, Amsterdam
2011 *From Trash to Treasure – Vom Wert des Wertlosen in der Kunst*, Kunsthalle zu Kiel, Kiel (G)
2009 *Artists from the 60s*, The Mayor Gallery, London (G)
2007 Staatliches Museum Schwerin
2006 *ZERO* – Musée d´Art moderne de Saint-Etienne (G)
*ZERO – Internationale Künstler-Avantgarde der 50er/60er Jahre*, Museum Kunstpalast, Düsseldorf (G)
2003 *The Daimler Chrysler Collection*, ZKM | Zentrum für Kunst und Medientechnologie Karlsruhe, Karlsruhe (G)
1998 Kunstraum Potsdam
1997 *Magie der Zahl*, Staatsgalerie Stuttgart, Stuttgart (G)
1993 *Die holländische Gruppe Nul*, Villa Merkel, Esslingen (G)
1989 Petersen Galerie, Berlin
1982 *Künster arbeiten mit Fotos*, Kunsthalle zu Kiel (G)
1978 *Museum des Geldes*, Kunsthalle Düsseldorf;
*Musée de l'Argent*, Centre Georges Pompidou, Paris (G)

1965 *Pop Art / Nouveau Realisme*, Museum des 20. Jahrhunderts, Wien | Vienna; Aakademie der Künste, Berlin (G)
1964 *Nieuw Realisten*, Gemeentemuseum, Den Haag | The Hague (G)
1962 *Nul*, Stedelijk Museum Amsterdam, Amsterdam (G)
*Anti-Peinture*, Hessenhuis, Antwerpen | Antwerp (G)
1961 *Avantgarde '61*, Städtisches Museum, Trier (G)
*Internationale Malerei 1960-'61*, Deutschordensschloss, Wolframs-Eschenbach (G)

(G) Gruppenausstellung | Group exhibition

# IMPRESSUM | COLOPHON

Diese Publikation erscheint anlässlich der Ausstellung:
**Jan Henderikse** – Zwischen ZERO und Pop Art: Arbeiten 1967 – 2017

This publication is published in conjunction with the exhibition:
**Jan Henderikse** – Between ZERO and Pop Art: Works 1967 – 2017

12. September – 31. Oktober 2017 | September 12th – October 31st, 2017, LEVY Galerie, Osterfeldstraße 6, 22529 Hamburg, Germany, Tel. + 49 – (0) 40 – 459188, Fax + 49 – (0) 40 – 447225, info@levy-galerie.de, www.levy-galerie.de

**Herausgeber | Editor:** Thomas Levy **Texte | Texts:** Antoon Melissen **Redaktion | Editing:** Marleen-Christine Linke, Helene Osbahr **Übersetzung (Engl. – Dt.) | Translation (Engl. – Germ.):** Belinda Grace Gardner **Kataloggestaltung | Graphic design:** Claas Möller, claasbooks.de, Hamburg **Fotografien | Photographs:** Christiaan Clauwers, Antwerpen | Antwerp
**Gesamtherstellung und Vertrieb | Printed and published by:**

**Kerber Verlag**
Windelsbleicher Straße 166 – 170
D-33659 Bielefeld, Germany
Tel. +49 – (0) 521 – 95008 – 10
Fax +49 – (0) 521 – 95008 – 88
info@kerberverlag.com

**Kerber, US Distribution, ARTBOOK | D. A. P.**
75 Broad Street, Suite 630
New York, NY 10004, USA
T: 001 – 212 – 6271999
F: 001 – 212 – 6279484

Die Deutsche Nationalbibliothek verzeichnet diese Publikation in der Deutschen Nationalbibliografie; detaillierte bibliografische Daten sind im Internet über: http://dnb.dnb.de abrufbar. | The Deutsche Nationalbibliothek holds a record of this publication in the Deutsche Nationalbibliografie; detailed bibliographical data can be found under: http://dnb.dnb.de.

KERBER-Publikationen werden weltweit in führenden Buchhandlungen und Museumsshops angeboten (Vertrieb in Europa, Asien, Nord- und Südamerika). | KERBER publications are available in selected bookstores and museum shops worldwide (distributed in Europe, Asia, South and North America).



**Danksagung | Acknowledgements** Unser besonderer Dank gilt Roland Janssen von der Galerie Schoots + van Duyse für seine vielfältige Unterstützung und Hilfe bei der Umsetzung des Kataloges und der Ausstellung. | Our special thanks go to Roland Janssen of Galerie Schoots + van Duyse for his manifold support throughout the process of realizing the catalogue and the exhibition.

ISBN 978-3-7356-0414-9 www.kerberverlag.com Printed in Germany